BE

Written by Greg Petri

Illustrated by Matthew Dowling

ISBN: 978-0-578-21198-5

Cover design by Matthew Dowling
All illustrations by Matthew Dowling
Layout design by Matthew Dowling

Edited by Christina E. Scannell

Printed in the United States of America

Published by 2B Creative Publishing

INTRODUCTION:

From the Artist

The illustrations in this book represent an attempt to better understand the world and my place in it. These creative efforts are a response to the busyness of the everyday. Life's frenetic pace often pulls me off course. The act of painting reminds me to slow down, exhale, and notice the beauty inhabiting the everyday world. In moments of artistic creation, perceptions become clear in the midst of heightened awareness of both the 'self' and the play of line, color, shape, and space unfolding on the canvas in front of me. The answer begins to emerge through art. I am most alive in the act of creation.

That is why the creative act is, in my mind, such an important, even spiritual experience. Making new things spurns into existence an inner part of the self to display in the physical world. Painting has always played a valuable role in my search for answers to life's big questions; what are we doing, and why are we here? It creates a quiet space for contemplation and reflection. This *BE* book, and the artwork on its pages, introduces the notion that, contrary to modern perception, lasting joy is found not in achieving a goal, but in the journey itself. The process of trying to answer those ultimate questions could, in fact, be the answer that is right in front of us. This book challenged me to see the world through a new lens, where gratitude for what I have replaces the nervous longing for what I lack. Everything I need is already here, especially when I'm creating art.

The BE Book is the culmination of Greg's vision of a world where awareness of the journey is celebrated and the triumphant return of the creative act is valued above all else. The making of something new is central to our existence; it's when we feel most alive. Making art is a way of reaching another plane of awareness, of life experience. The senses are heightened when consumed in an art moment. Nothing else matters in those moments. Time ceases to exist. It is escapism in its purest form. My hope is that, by reading this book, you are inspired to be 'in the moment', to unthink the vastness of a cluttered life ....and just BE.

Enjoy the book, and the peace that comes with noticing, and creating, beautiful things.

Sincerely,

Matt Dowling

With Gratitude

First to my mom and dad, whose unending belief in my artistic skills led to this moment. From an early drawing in the 5th grade of the Steve Miller Band, Book of Dreams album cover (My art career could have easily ended before it started when the drawing tragically got sucked up into a vacuum cleaner) to my almost thirty year career as an art educator, to my work as a muralist, their unwavering support of their son's involvement in the arts made this book possible.

I want to thank Greg Petri for his belief in a creative spirit that often lacks confidence in its abilities. His indomitable positive energy instilled a belief in my ability to add some life to this book's previous edition, *Fairies in the Trees.* Never once did Greg permit me to doubt the quality of my work, his writing, or the marriage of the two that would become, *BE.*

Finally, I want the world to know how much I appreciate the unwavering support and love of my best friend and wife, Stacey (aka 'Schmoopy'). She is an inspiration to me and our two wonderful children, providing a role model of passion and persistence in whatever she does. It was her stubborn insistence that I meet with Greg that led to the publication of this book. She has always believed in my abilities as an artist and designer, providing a voice of encouragement that helped guide me through the many challenges presented by this project. It was Stacey who saw the potential of what Greg and I could accomplish together. Just look what we've done!

A Personal Note From the Author

After many years on this planet, meeting thousands and thousands of people, running my own business, an alternative chamber of commerce, it seems to me, what every single human being wants is sustained happiness, peace and contentment. *The **BE** Book*, is a guide to this personal awakening and true happiness.

How do I know these things? Because this book was written in one month (a cosmic download) from an experience I had that lasted weeks, many call it a Satori, others an epiphany, whatever it's called, it has left me with residual peace that has never left.

I believe this book will be a value and a guide for many generations to come in 100, 500, even 1,000's of years from now.

This book ***BE*** is the heirloom copy that can be handed down from generation to generation. Many young people are being inspired by this book. People who seek actual truth and more meaning in their lives have found peace and wisdom in its artful expression. Those who just need a reminder are also delighted by *The **BE** Book*.

My hope is that you enjoy it, and it makes you smile and it helps you realize that life, your life, is truly a gift. *The **BE** Book* can open up new discoveries, unseen worlds and insights for every single person on this earth. But more than that - use this as a backroad guide to enjoy deeply every moment of the rest of your proverbial life.

Enjoy the lightness, the illumination, and the unique art in this book...so simply called ***BE***. It can (if you are open to it) let you see, be and discover more awareness, joy, bliss and happiness...always.

Greg Petri, Author, Speaker and Entrepreneur

This book is dedicated to those who seek the

Actual Truth!

For [this book] is so simple, it is difficult to understand.

The path so easy,

Few can follow it.

Or as Lao Tzu wrote around 500 B.C. ...

My words are very easy to understand

and very easy to put into practice.

Yet no one in the world can understand them or

put them into practice.

CONTENTS

CONTENTS

Chapter 1

Seeing Through the Illusion

Many have talked of it, Alan Watts, Ken Wilber, the masters, the Buddha, Lao Tzu, Jesus, talked of the illusion we partake in, dwell on, find ourselves caught in like being between the dawn and the dusk, on a merry-go-round going 'round and 'round.

So eloquently many have explained it, pointed it out — poets, artists, sages, men of the mind like Jung and Fromm, the mystics and fantastics like Castaneda — but seldom do we find methodology for breaking free of this illusion we are living.

The West is in desperate need of freeing itself of the chains, finding paths that coincide, work, that unravel the bits of illusions forming and help us find not only meaning in the recurring dreams we are part of but how to let go. So give up the religions and the ideologies. Find an all-encompassing spirituality that works, not just in the Sunday churches, not because we blindly follow the advice of some minister. Be careful to believe men or women of seemingly insight and power, or those who sprinkle down their precious gifts on us lowly of evolved on the totem pole of reality.

Those who we may look up to — could be bosses, men of money, the religiously fervent, those that might have a thread of evidence of the nature of the world, the seers, the ones we've read, whoever — they are all but guideposts.

All of us are already enlightened beyond measure, it is that our awareness just needs to catch up.

It really is a very personal and fantastic journey, taken a step at a time, but not only that, we need to somehow integrate, incorporate, delineate that path we have chosen.

It has been said, there are many paths that will get us to the same end: to God, to the promised land, to where there is no more perceived suffering, to our inner peace.

I say there is only one path and that path is of such a personal nature, that we liken it to "the many."

I'm sure there have been numerous times that you have felt caught in the eternal moment, that time is an illusion, and that you are a spiritual being, part of the ethereal, or cosmic, or divine matter that makes up life. It could be a sensation, a moment at the beach where reality seems to bypass the trivial and you enter the core, or maybe a piece of poetry that may have moved you, or a lover that may have reflected back to you your own soul—a sensation: Call it spiritual experiences, the divine finally making itself evident...whatever. These are the experiences we crave, because we do feel separation, the distancing of ourselves from ourselves and from God.

Ultimately, poetically, artistically, universally, absolutely it is our destiny and our free will or lack of both (or mixture of both) that we should get to this source, the source which is peace, is God, is

Ultimately, poetically, artistically, universally, absolutely it is our destiny and our free will or lack of both (or mixture of both) that we should get to this source, the source which is peace, is God, is a truth that cannot be justified, or intellectualized, a spot in ourselves that is eternal, feels right...that is all we are ever trying to do. The rest are games of a lesser God, ways of placating our sorrow from being away from the source, from God, from the truest part of ourselves that is exactly everything all at once.

The problem with most books, most philosophies, most espoused ways, is there is contained within them the ritual, the leaps of faith that need to be accepted, like reading an astrology chart and seeing how it applies to this situation — believing each and every word, or chanting a mantra to get to a state of non-thought, or kneeling and praying and hoping this shall find God, and He is magnanimous enough to respond, to intervene in our quiet desperation.

There is a stripping away of this ritual, these leaps of faith and not losing any of the magic or mystery, the awe inspiring life force that is within us, that is actually all of us. So often we are caught up in images, imaginations, satyrs and dragons flying through the devastation of some Irish village where the Loch Ness monster sets a picnic table for the knights and rogues and the princesses who have been so much in distress of late.

We love our myth, our fantasies, should we say our illusions - they are like blankets to keep us warm.

This book shall be how to give up our illusions and still keep our incredible awareness of that which is so fantastic that we can but imagine its power, its source, its facets. We should never lose our awe of this world, just our misrepresentations, our rituals, our illusions of what we think reality could be.

Fantasy is nothing but an extrapolation of this awe, a prediction of, better said an invention from, the source of the ultimate mystery, because we have no way to explain that which cannot be categorized.

This is a starting point, a springboard, actual directives to finding the core of our existence, so we never, ever have to go back to our addictions, our illusions, our games of a boxed-in God again.

BE

Chapter 2

First Precept

You are already enlightened.

We are basking, bathing in the eternal moment and if we stop the thoughts, look upon the beauty of this world, see, then it becomes obvious we are eternal, we are already enlightened.

There is an absolute, unchanging, infinite part to what we think is a universe of things — it is but a whole. When we understand this, that we are this huge thing, these things, then we find peace. It's like taking a train to nowhere and understanding you've already arrived, no need for tickets.

From youth, we are indoctrinated to get somewhere, to get more, to go to McDonalds, to have something fun to do, to look forward to, to be so very agitated and impatient with each moment. This is, of course, the illusion.

How can you get to somewhere when you are already there?

How can you get to, travel to some point you want to attain when that point is in your pocket?

So the first precept is that we are all enlightened; we just need to realize this truth, we merely need to sit and see, be.

But so many say: "Hey, there is so much I want, so much to get, to attain, to evolve to, to become, so many places to go, so many people to get to know."

And I think so many truly believe that enlightenment is some kind of grueling journey, a hard and rugged journey that takes us to the depths and then, perhaps after years, and many believe, after lifetimes of suffering and cleansing pain, finally we might get a glimpse or two of nirvana: Brahma, human spiritual satori, ultimate understanding.

This is, again, the same concept that puts it out there on a linear path. This is not so! It can all be had in a nanosecond, in a flash, an epiphany, in a releasing of the moment into the moment into the moment — a process that seems to go on but is not in any sort of actually movement.

The dissatisfaction, the turmoil, the impatience, the desires to get more, to be secure, to be somewhere else (like on a perceived, upcoming vacation), to be with someone else, to be over there, instead of right here...this is the separation.

As soon as we figure out this is the illusion, then we can have exactly what we are looking for, and for all beings, it is contentment, inner peace, the state of bliss that cannot be ripped away by a whim or other people's reactions.

I really cannot believe that every single human is not looking for the same thing: inner contentment! But maybe some are seeking gold, fame, intimacy...alas, they, too, will — at some distant moment — realize the illusion that has them by the balls.

So many have talked of it, this linear timeline that seems so real: You get up, go to work, the sun goes down and some day, you are old and die.

Once we understand that this linear timeline is a learned illusion, then we can sit fat and happy in the eternal moment that is happening everywhere all at once, and thus be so blissful as we run through, watch, the drama of life.

It really is as simple as realizing that we are eternal beings in the eternal moment and that the rest is some manufactured way of looking at how we have trained ourselves as a culture, as a people, to view the passing of life, and time.

So we are completely enlightened. And if we feel not so, seem not, it is simply our desire to have more, or to be caught in some traumatic past experience that keeps us in patterns of existence. Like we are looking to have a heaven or future that really never arrives, waiting for a late train and always looking at our watch, wanting spring to finally come so that we forget to enjoy the winter, thinking we can (by mere achievement) attain our goals. Get more things, more money, more fame or prestige, thus creating our very own happiness that forever eludes us. This illusion must be dispelled for us to enter into, and remain in, the state of constant, unchanging, eternal bliss...it is so! And so many have said it before, it is nothing new.

Chapter 3

First Logical Step

The question is that if we are all enlightened, why in God's name do we not feel enlightened? What has created the separateness, this illusory sensation, the problems we are entangled in?

From birth we have been conditioned by parents who were conditioned by their parents who were conditioned by the culture, the society, that we have needed to get somewhere, be someone, find our calling, our talents, our passions, become a doctor, a police officer, a pilot, a minister, an educated person...who knows who we have been driven to become.

Socially we've been chopped up into separate entities, have thus found roles to play that have their own rules, instead of being the enlightened beings we were born to be.

Let's say John has found his way, after years of struggle and hard work, into a major corporation and is an upper level manager, and he takes the job so seriously, and it comes with some power to influence, to dictate, to tell others what to do, so that he internalizes that job, becomes the job, the roles he is shown how to play, becomes a jerk, is now the boss who can delegate and walk around as if he is someone more important than rest of the lowly drones because he has "achieved" this status of power from this artificial world of "the company."

It seems real to John. He has loyalty to company X and actually is proud of himself for his salary, his position, his title, loves this power over people. And for some reason, they actually do what he tells them, usually because they too are participants in this fantasy, want to become like John and, someday (in the rosy future) have John's title and power so they too can be more than they believe they already are, and the illusion goes 'round and 'round.

Then what happens? After many years of conditioning himself "to be" the roles he plays, he finally retires, the company forgets about him, and this role is stripped away, and he feels like a shell: no power, no title, no one to tell what to do...he is lost in the Who am I dilemma.

We are all conditioned to be, to act, to think, to believe, to seem...a certain way. And how can we overcome this paradox, this conditioning that pervades so much of what we call social order? How can we get outside that which we believe we are? How can we go beyond who we've been taught we are?

First, we must realize all that we think, the actual process of thinking is the illusion, all that goes in and out of our minds is what is propagating this separateness.

Deepak Chopra has said, though it has been said by many others (many who teach meditation): "Stop the thoughts." Once we concentrate on just the present, just what is unraveling in front of our eyes, just see to see, non-judgmentally looking at people, things, others, or as Lao Tzu would say, the

10,000 Things, then we can dispel the illusion that traps us in subcultures, roles, into groups, into nations, societies, into separate little selfish entities trying so hard to grab more for ourselves.

We have conditioned ourselves to love our very precious thoughts, to be convinced that our thoughts are so true, so real, when they are but shadows of things, phantoms, usually given to us like milk in a bottle by the culture or subculture, and we don't even know we have adopted them, and instead actually think: "Ah, this thought here, this juicy one, is mine. It is original. I figured this out all by myself: I must have a mortgage, a family, and a career in a big company (or whatever)...I know exactly what I want to do."

We have been trained to live in our minds, to think a lot and plan, to justify, rationalize our perceived world, all in our own minds, to justify our own reactions and fleeting emotions. Yet they are usually recurring patterns of emotions that are trapped inside, that we actually live in a world of illusion, artificially made up by our own thoughts about it.

Once we think about a thing, once we abstract, then that thing becomes false. Once we try to explain a thing, a situation, it becomes false. Your thinking makes a dualism between you and the thing you are thinking about; thus, separation; thus, an illusory world.

Let's say Joe is on the front lawn. It is new spring, the world is full of birds singing, sunshine that is soft, warm, incredibly wondrous, and the sky is blue and the air sweet, fresh, with a slight cool breeze rustling old leaves caught in the flower beds. But Joe notices none of this because he is worried about some project at work, and is thinking about how the boss was so mean to him about not getting this certain project done on time and he is, thus, stuck in "the thinking about something" that is not real. He misses the entire wondrous reality happening.

Sure this may seem simple enough, but how many times a day can we catch ourselves in this abstract world of thinking?

Stop and smell the roses. Better said: "Stop your thoughts and always smell the roses, smell everything. Look! See! Be!"

As we begin to train our minds to be completely in the present, to see the keys on the keyboard as we write instead of abstracting into this world of thoughts that generates separating emotions and beliefs, then we finesse our eternalness, that we are forever beings, not merely believe we are, or convince ourselves of this, or have faith that it is so, but can actually start to intuitively yet deeply realize we live in the eternal moment and are eternal — part of God — and just as energy cannot be destroyed, we also cannot be destroyed, instead can only change forms, find our ways back to the All-ness, back to God.

So the first step in becoming, realizing we already are enlightened beings, is to deeply know that everything we need is right here, in this burgeoning present moment and that if we simply acknowledge this, stay in the present, stop abstracting and creating an illusionary world in our own minds, then we can feel, sense, be this universal everything-ness that is happening everywhere, all at once. We can feel and act with this power.

And what is truly beautiful about this truth is that it takes no belief, no leap of faith, no formal training, no ritual, no religious fanaticism, no education to do it.

Simply do it and see the results, or see how there are no results, just an eternal moment without a past or a future to get us crazy. Thus, it is a commonsense, real approach to finding the peace we have so longed and looked for.

For our entire lives we have trained ourselves to live in some illusionary future, to get somewhere, to be someone else, to find something, to seek something, to create our own reality, to justify our way of living.

It takes time, or practice, to keep the mind in the present. For true peace we must realize the abstractions, fun and entertaining or devastating as they might appear to be, they are really the source of our separateness, the suffering point that we need to comprehend so as to go beyond the patterns and the illusions.

All the bliss we need is here, right now, in this present moment. Every answer, every perplexity, all that we have been looking for is right here; not in our lover's eyes, not in some future vacation, or some meaningful experience that has happened or will happen, for the meaningful experience is happening right now. Get out of the patterns of social convention, their misrepresentations of reality, and thus, find actual freedom, an eternal place to reside and spin truth around ourselves and be content.

Chapter 4

Kill The Buddha

There is an old Buddhist saying, "If you see the Buddha on the road, kill him." So I've taken this to mean that there is no outward Buddha, no master who you should give up your enlightenment to. No one can take you to where you must take yourself.

So often we are looking for the leader, be them political, religious, the wise man on the right path who can tell us the correct way, tell us the truth, give us that which, somehow, we have convinced ourselves we lack. This is the illusion. And sometimes the biggest illusion, the greatest hypocrisy, is surrounding those who will not acknowledge that they are lacking, unhappy, when they are, inside, full of ego, full of themselves.

All that we need to know is within us, can be tapped into without the rigorous training of the monks sitting on a rock amidst some Himalayan mountain. We have within us the enlightenment we need, the peace of heart, the truth, we do not need to look for it elsewhere. There is no elsewhere. To think there is, is again, the fallacy.

Emerson said books should be to inspire. And, of course, as Tara Singh has said: "True words can ring true," can motivate us to be, to see, they can point to, allude to...and that is about all they can do...point to, leave a marker.

We are, or at least seem to be, on a personal journey home, and we have the roadmaps inside our spirit, inside our souls, and can traverse all these seemingly rugged valleys and mountains, the desolate paths. We can so easily find our way if we quit looking for someone to tell us which path, direction, which way to go.

A wondrous women wrote a tiny little book called The Peace Pilgrim. It was all about how to create and find peace. And in this special book she wrote that one day she woke up and there were no more valleys, no more suffering or inner strife. She had found the mountain tops and stayed there for the rest of her peaceful life.

Even the Buddha after attaining his enlightenment was asked to tell of it, show them the way. He could do no more than hold up a flower. No words, no explanations could say or teach it, for it was, is, shall always be here all the time. This is all such an incredible simplicity that we seem to have an amazingly hard time trying to understand it. We must never delude ourselves into thinking there is some place to get to.

It is here with all of us, all of the time.

And the Hare Krishna's (who have such a bad proselytizing reputation of accosting people in airports years ago) sing, and chant, and all they are doing is praying to God who is with us each moment of each breath we take. Read the Bhagavad Gita, it is mostly about this. The more we dwell on this God-ness surrounding us, and understand this simple truth, the easier it is to be blissful without dogma or ritual, without professed religion. But Alan Watts once quoted a Chinese proverb: "Do not swat the fly on your friend's head with a hatchet." Be careful how you choose to convince people of what they should know.

Of course there are many people to admire, to honor in their beauty, their contributions to this sojourn, and we must humble ourselves to some great ones who can rip away part of the illusion for us, and I'm sure they laugh as we struggle where they might've been long ago, but ultimately it is a personal journey and we have all the tools, all the depth, all the reality to become as cosmic, as enlightened as we choose. Though, sad as it may seem, many do not care or choose to find their bliss — at least from our perspectives.

So this book may not be an actual instruction of how to find our bliss, but it is a bit more than a poetic pointing, suggestions that have worked for me whereas I must admit I am most usually blissful, peaceful and content.

Ultimately, we all find the way to our peace. Some find it sooner than others, some in their twenties, some after forty years, some in their dying last breath, but we shall find that which we sometimes believe cannot be found.

Again, all that we seek is not in the explaining, or as Ken Wilber calls it, "the mapping out of reality." There is the actual mountain and then there are maps of this mountain. We so often are in the mental mapping of reality with our thoughts, our explanations. We can talk until we are blue in the face, until the cows come home, until there is nothing left to say. It is the moment, the pulling back from our abstracting, from this mental jump roping that will bring us to the unending bliss that we seek.

In fact, I wonder so often why even write about it, for it is almost futile because that which we so eloquently may be able to describe, that which we may so intricately dissect is still just the mapping. Our words are, in a way, hollow. But it is fun, and we should do what is fun, follow our bliss.

All the great masters did try to explain it, and it helps to remind ourselves that there is a constant, a reality, an eternal. It helps us to realize we are not mad, we are genuinely understanding something that others have also come across.

I was driving around in Boulder and saw a bumper sticker, a tiny map. It read: Life is the school. Love is the lesson. And maybe we should look at it as simply as this.

And, yet, there are times words can inspire, or remind us of the things we already know deep inside. What I write about is nothing new, nothing that so many probably have not already thought about, touched upon. But again, it is worth reminding ourselves of these things, as we so often get lost in the getting there, in our jobs, our wanting so badly a "secure" or happy future that will never, ever arrive unless we arrive and stay first in this powerful, complete, eternal present moment. And once we arrive, then we can take any journey that we want to, we can go anywhere, loosen up the self-inflicted emotions and chains and walk to the top of the mountain because that is as good as it all gets. We, thus, can smile at the shy, purple flowers that begin to grow by the drain pipe as the spring days get longer and longer, and we can witness our truth in the coolness of an evening breeze, slip into a state of bliss and remain there forever without having to come back down to the valleys, the pettiness of the thrashing around of ideas, emotions, desires, of getting somewhere...ever again.

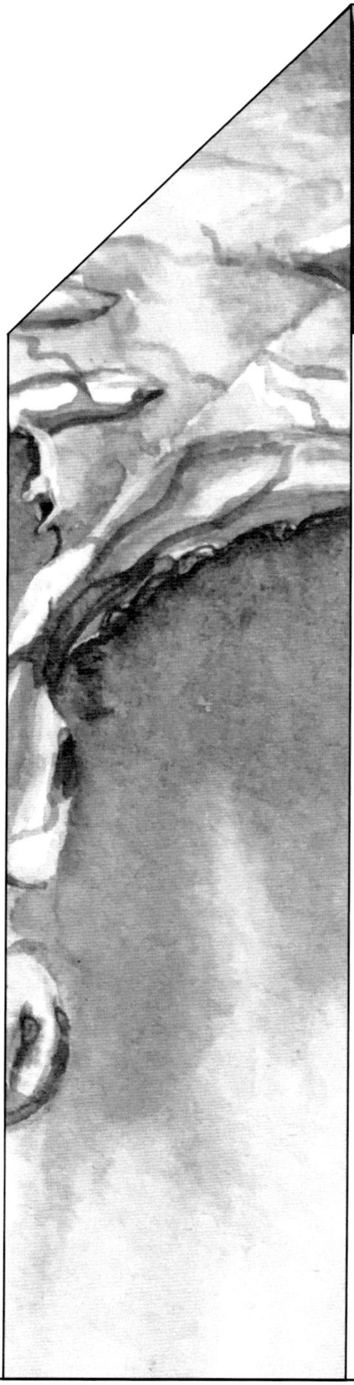

BE

Chapter 5

The Bliss Factor

What else can there be than the bliss factor? To be so incredibly at peace, so content, so at oneness with the world that we emanate a security without any need of security, and we know this complete bliss no matter what the drama seems to be going on around us...this is what we can all have.

Bliss is not exactly happiness, as most emotions must have their opposite: happy/sad, love/hate...no, bliss is more like a residing in the universal truth, in the present, being in the moment and, somehow, consciously knowing that there is no more, nowhere to get to, no heaven above, no hell below, no fear, no demons chasing us, no thoughts or emotions that can overwhelm or disturb us. This state is close enough to enlightenment, is the state where enlightened realizations happen. Thus, we start to see through the patterns of behavior, start to become wise, understand the things we never even conceived of.

For example, I love my nine-year-old son dearly, but at times he would react, not listen, get mad when I told him what to do, argue with me, lash out and I would be adamant, serious about him not getting mad, about him listening and obeying me. I'd get angry trying to force him not to argue with me, and at times I would get so enraged that he was getting angry at me. I thought, "Hey, I'll teach him never to get upset at me by getting upset at him...showing him who is the real boss. I actually thought "anger for anger" would teach.

But, by staying in states of bliss, I have realized that he can only learn love with love, can only stay in his anger if I show him anger. I needed to teach him with love not to be angry, that he was creating his own anger.

Simple yet insightful little things like this start to happen. We come to understand, comprehend things as they are, not as we have chosen to react to them or rationalize them in our routinely illusory way.

Another realization is about the thoughts we have. They are not involuntary reactions like breathing, or the beating of our own hearts. We should and can choose to think when we want to instead of letting our thoughts become locusts in our head flitting about like unwanted, usually, passersby, but more like tools to use, to guide, even to inspire. The more aware we are of each and every thought as it comes to us, creates an emotion and leaves, the more we shall reside in the state of bliss. We must own our own thoughts; they are created by us; we let them fly wildly by, no one else but us...except when we are being receptive to another's thoughts (like telepathy).

Thinking is something that will be discussed in more depth.

But, think about this: Isn't it all we really want out of life, to be in a constant state of bliss or

But, think about this: Isn't it all we really want out of life, to be in a constant state of bliss or peace, where the circumstances of our lives do not interfere with our contentment, where we can roll with the punches, be the forever, a steadily burning candle in any soft or violent wind?

So often we sabotage our peace, are too excited and for some reason, think or act as if there must be more, or think this cannot be so good, and thus find ways to destroy our peace with more searching, more wanting of things, more success, or thinking there must be more.

There is no more. Once we understand the Buddha and the flower, love thy neighbor as ourselves, because, as Alan Watts proposed: "We are our neighbors. We are all God." So what we are seeing at any aware moment is God anyway, is ourselves. There is nothing to be afraid of, nothing to compete with, nothing to feel separate or apart from.

This state of bliss is deeply knowing we are in the eternal moment, and that all things are with us, and that there is an eternity here to work with. No rush. No maddening "getting there." No wishing upon a star to get something we have always wanted.

Many realize it's our desire that confounds, that hangs us by our necks. It's our desires that convolute, pollute, make us so frantic in the present moment, create such a dissatisfied state of affairs.

The late Ken Keyes had a whole school of happiness. His school at Coos Bay, Oregon was dedicated to getting people to understand this simple point: "Up-level all your desires to preferences." Meaning, if you merely prefer to get what you want, then you are not addicted to the result, to what you somehow believe you must have to be fulfilled.

Desire is nothing but a wish for a future, a conscious decision to get more for the self (and Ken Wilber explains it so thoroughly that there is no future nor self). This or any desire immediately separates the self from the present and creates the suffering, the illusion that there is somewhere to get to. It cannot be done except in the neurosis of our own minds. Desire, the seven deadly sins, of lust and greed and avarice and so on are simply ideas that we can have something better, more rewarding in the future. Yet, if we simply realize this is the basis of all illusion then the bliss factor happens. We are at one, at peace, having so much fun just being right here, right now, and enjoying the ride.

There seems to have been a handful of great sages down through the ages, all have understood the Tao, the flow, God, this simple but so powerful truth. Now, with the world in disrepair, where so many greedy little humans have gone about polluting, consuming, getting, seeking, we do not need a handful of Jesuses but a million, a 100 million of enlightened beings to guide us into (or at least keep reminding us of) these states of bliss, where we can begin to see through the illusion of rules and laws, of getting more things, finding some "other Utopia" that we so much think we need to get to.

Part of the lack of bliss is that we have been conditioned, especially by a Western social brainwashing that we must live a certain lifestyle, have so many things, so much money, IRAs, two cars, things, more things, prestige, careers. But along with the things we also have lives that become too full, so stressed, so off balance, so out of sorts that we become tired, over worked, fretful, oh-so-worried about not being able to pay for all our things. There is a simple solution here: Need less, want less, consume less. The old saying of live simply so others can simply live might apply here.

But so many argue, "I have this job. I must do what I'm told." I say quit your job. "But, but I will lose my pension, my security." I say you are losing right now, your peace. If any of our lives are too full, it is our responsibility to trim them down, to find a pace that is right for us, relaxed, but with possibilities.

Want less, need less, be satisfied in the present, and all will be with you. There is no need to judge what we have by what others have, no need to climb the social ladder, because at the top it is usually a bunch of confused and frantic people who have sacrificed the present (and their

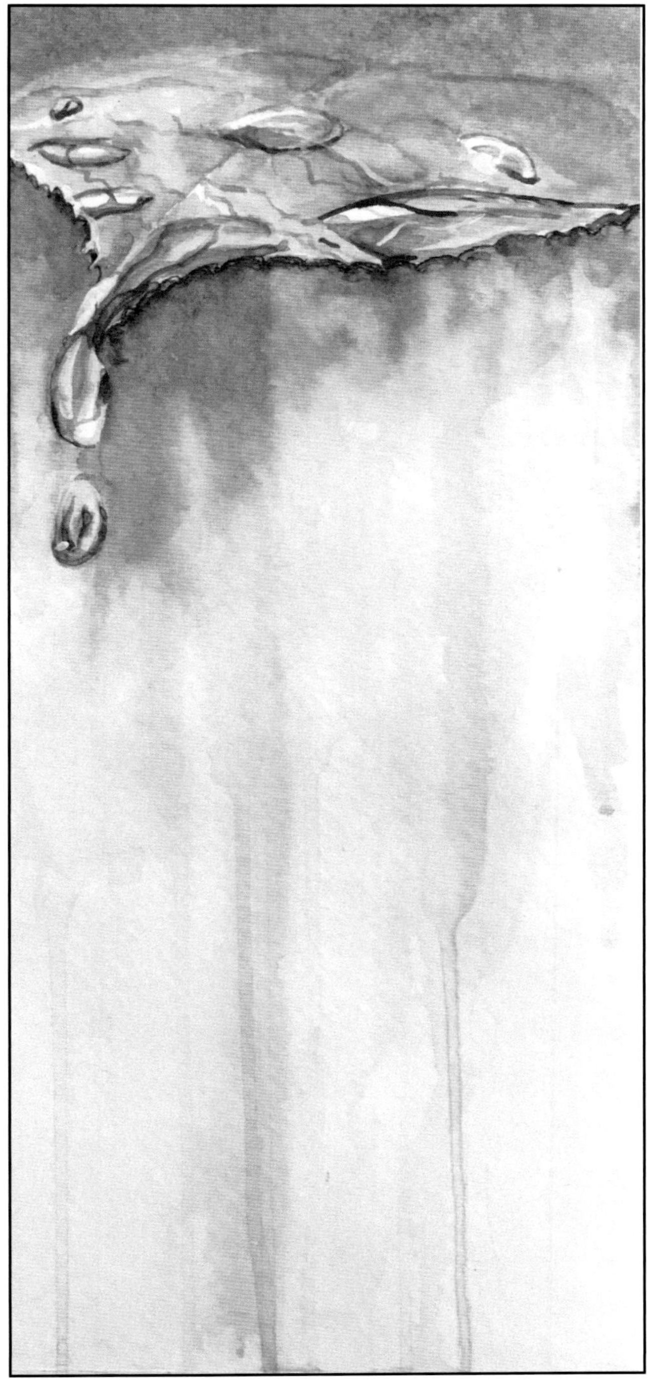

sanity) in order to climb so high into this propagated illusion.

The bliss factor is real, extremely and perfectly real, like cake for all to eat, like blue sky for all of us to share, like the sifting of the wind through the senses, or the perfect day that lasts forever. It is right here, right now, no exceptions.

BE

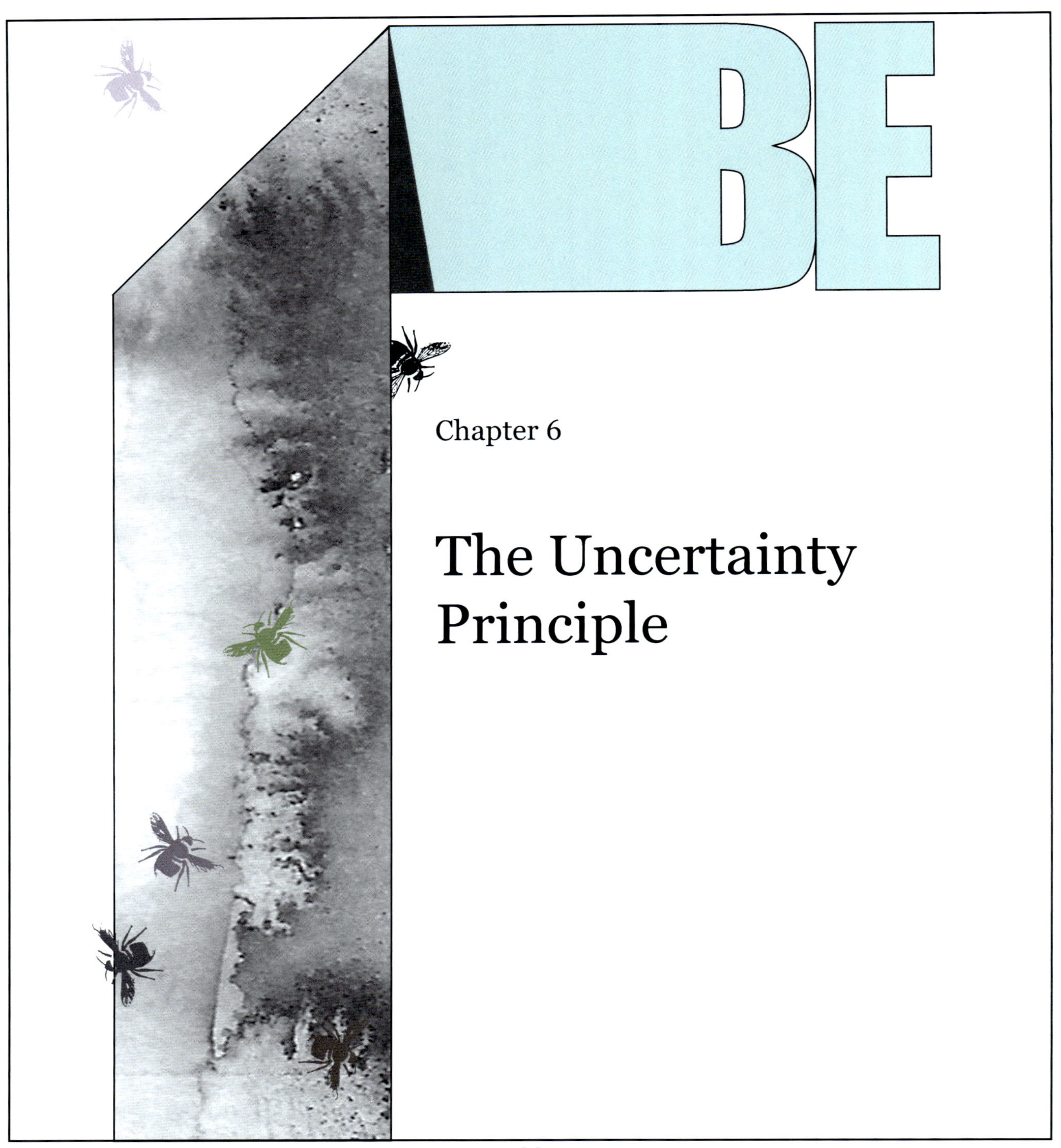

Chapter 6

The Uncertainty Principle

When it comes to beliefs, ideas, abstractions, things we have been taught to believe, there is always, at least should be, the possibility that the specific idea, thought, belief is not true, partially true, completely false, part of this illusion we keep speaking of.

If we don't realize that there is always present this element of uncertainty, then we become affixed on a thing, an idea, a way. Uncertainty lets us be open, fluid, at least entertain other points of view.

It is so easy in any of our abstractions to take them as absolute truth, as fact in this world of mental fiction. The real truth is that all thought is fiction. And if we must pick a certainty, one absolute, it is that there is one giant universe and we are part of it. But even this can be broken, disturbed by concepts like the Many Worlds Theory (multiple universes happening at one time), and so on. The only certainty I have found is that there is God everywhere and there is an eternal moment that is going on and on and we have the absolute potential — or call it the option — to be, at all times, peaceful and blissful.

But what if this idea is false, what if this, too, is an illusion fit snugly inside our limited view of the world? Uncertainty!

For example, supposedly the world was created 10 to 15 billion years ago, and when the Big Bang happened, it created billions of these tiny black holes all over, not only this galaxy but the hundreds upon thousands of other galaxies, and this space extends to some kind of universe perhaps within itself and we can — in the astrophysics way — realize there is just too much to even possibly comprehend, such incredible chasms to cross that we cannot even come close to imagining the things that are going on in other parts of this universe. But we, here on little planet earth, in our incredibly intellectual heyday, with all this stupendous mental acuity, workable technologies, have figured it all out...we "know"...but they are merely personal soliloquies we project into the void, constructs over reality. So absurd.

There is no figuring it out, only a level of peace we can get in sync with.

The uncertainty principle is the basis of our ability to be open-minded, to not attach ourselves to one specific, alienating philosophy, idea, set of ideas, religious fervor or flavor, one ideology that immediately separates us from other supposedly opposing, contrary ideologies.

We need to always be uncertain about what thoughts themselves can get us to, but perhaps we should never be uncertain about the joy, the emanations we sense in our beings, our oneness feelings of lasting peace.

And yet if we believe we must always be in state of bliss we again are forming, conceptualizing about what we think is the right way to be, to act, trying so hard to suppress our anger, our frustrations, our pain, whatever may be the appropriate and actual feelings or emotional responses we are having.

Uncertainty is not as unstable, as insecure as it may seem. It is simply a basis for leaving the door open instead of slamming it shut, letting our minds be free to meander in the twilight and explore, rather than sucking on one chicken bone until it pops.

So many are so certain of the trinity, of the Buddhist way, of this and that, of the meaning of a certain Zen koan, of grandmother's advice.

Of course, there are some things that seem to pervade all higher thoughts and levels: bliss, love, giving, balance, truth, God, Godhead, nirvana, Brahma, eternity, infinity, cosmic and undulating energy, flux, and so on. But how we interpret any of this we must leave in the reality of uncertainty. This way, anything we read, any seer of the absolute truth can be questioned, not taken as the one and only incredible truth.

We as humans need to have our perceptions, our language to explain, our filters through which something that may be pure and true and absolute is sifted. Our ideas always lose something in interpretation, in the words that we use.

Read any of the great thinkers and they all basically say, point to the same things just in different nomenclature of the times of their specific training.

It all is, again, just the pointing to, nothing else; not the actual things in themselves, not the actual thing itself.

So before we bite hard on any particular belief, style of thinking, philosophy of living, before we become adamant in our right-ness, our point, a view that is so profound...just for an instant, maybe we should think that it could be completely off base, wrong, or at least incomplete, lacking, anemic in its vitalness, merely a facet, a door opening up into a room of many other doors where bigger rooms are found.

This is important if we are to see more of the connective-ness of life, if we are to accept, understand, see through the illusion that we are always trying so hard to form around our perceptions like ice trying to form around a cool pool of perfection. It is our way to make that which is forever in motion static, to make our certainty become solid, when it could be, maybe should be, like a river:

gentle,

going around the big rocks,

timeless in its ebb and flow...

...washing through our perceptions.

BE

Chapter 7

Inner Peace

Though some may not admit it, may want to cloud this precept with words, ideas, language that distorts, and many are too busy, too confused to even acknowledge it, and most don't have it so cannot envision it...we all want inner peace, an understanding that all is okay, that there is no more digging, pushing and striving for something.

Ken Wilber calls it the transpersonal level when/where you actually realize you are everything — watching everything, still a slight split, but when you become in actuality everything, you rest in the eternal mind, which most would call God. Thus, we are not part of God, we are not an image of God, we are not touched by the holy spirit. Rather, we are the holy spirit, we are God, we are the essence, the quintessence of all things and then we finally realize, call it through satori, realization, understanding, that we are all things and we reside in eternity — a place we have so long sought after.

This is inner peace, no mistaking it. There is no longer an illusion, no feeling of separation, no more getting there. No more getting anywhere. All thoughts become, all thinking is, illusion. All beliefs are merely conjured up "beliefs." Most often, we make them up as we go.

At this place, there is no place. It is like trying to explain to a blind man that light exists, or to define the most intricate and sweet music to those born deaf.

Words become a handful of bullets made of Play-Doh trying to be shoved into a plastic gun to go hunting quail.

It all becomes a mesh, a net, as in Zen: "The bottom falls out of the bucket." There is no more getting here, there, anywhere.

We all desire inner peace at a soul level, at a deeper level, at some level, and we should laugh as we run around striving for this and that, getting things, playing the games we have so very well been taught by a society that is so out of whack, so deranged. But so many keep playing, thinking one day, one sweet, long and wonderful day, I will have all my sticks in a row. I will have enough money, my sex life will be perfect, the rain will be soft and warm, my pension will kick in and I won't have to work and this and that and more this and that and it is all a societal drama created by the many who have gone before us who didn't know, didn't get it.

None of it is real. We are already at peace. We are already there. And there is no getting there.

But trying to explain this to someone who is not there, who has never been there, appears as if we are talking in riddles; mystics with chronic delusions. But, this is the absolute, certain, complete, incredible, settling and pure peace that there is and always will be.

Inner peace is simply coming to the realization that there is no place to run. In fact, when we do run, we are not moving; or as Lao Tzu wrote, non-action, action without action, doing without doing, purity in motion, effortless effort, getting there but never going anywhere because, at our deepest level, we realize we are, have always been, will always be "there."

So many have talked of this, in perhaps a different clarity, but I do think many have found this, many simple and ordinary people have found this, understand this, and they don't say or feel a need to say, or to explain it.

"Those who know don't say. Those who say don't know." But I must add, those who know and try to say appear to be those who don't know unless, of course, you, who is reading it, hearing it, knows...and then you go: "Hey, I get it. I got it. He does make sense..." even though it seems to be (to the many) absurdity on a stick, languid words trying to reach an end, the laughing of madmen in a corner.

It is not. Reality is simple: When you or I realize it in the deepest parts of who we are, that we are actually everything and this feeling will not go away, then it is not fleeting, it stays with us. Then and always then, we are at peace and can do whatever it is we would like. There are no more social rituals to entertain or chain us. We can climb a mountain, live with our aged mother, work just as hard as we did before, we can and do have complete freedom with or without money, without the snare of any greed, lust, avarice, jealousy, envy, no comparing ourselves to others, no feelings of belittlement because we have a gaping hole in our Levi's as we are talking with the woman who just stepped from the new and shiny Mercedes.

Inner peace is realizing, as the Peace Pilgrim, that there are no more valleys to descend to, no more devils and demons to flee from, to fight off, to wrestle. We finally have a settled and calm understanding that all pleasure and tragedy is but a simple drama that we can usually watch from a detached point of view, or a state of non-involvement, and then understand we are the drama, but it has no devastating effect on us. We are witnessing this play. We are the play, but after all, "Hey...it is just a play."

A young disciple once asked his master, "Why, oh wise master, why is there so much evilness in the world?" And the master replied: "It thickens the plot."

Lao Tzu wrote: "If you can laugh at it, it is the Way." It is the light and feathery feelings of inner peace, of understanding. It is like a cosmic joke and we finally get it, get the punch line. This is what becomes so incredibly amusing.

A dear friend of mine (a lawyer in Phoenix) and I were talking. He had been so frustrated, so broke, very lonely for so long, but he was also one of the most caring, loving, gentle humans whom I'd ever met. And as I tried to explain this thing about bliss and inner peace to him, he said, "Isn't that like what the Hindus believe in, nirvana, this blissfulness?" I said, "Exactly. It is all about bliss." And he added, "I'm always blissful when I am drunk." I laughed. What else can any of us do but laugh. The problem was that he was completely serious, absolutely serious. My poor friend. Yet, I always smile when I think of what a gentle soul he is...his gentleness is all he will ever need, he just needs to realize it.

All any of us really wants is inner peace. This is so true. If only more would, in their guts, in the essence of their beings, understand it is so very and easily possible to have, then we would be able to transcend the world by becoming the entire world. And the goal to become enlightened, to become God, to be saved, and even to become the world becomes so off-based, because we cannot become what we already are, what we have always been.

It is not that we do not have inner peace, it is that we do not realize we have inner peace. It is so much so a satori, a flash of insight into the ultimate workings of the universe, but the flash does not dissipate. And when all the frantic people stop looking...and see, and when all the mean people stop professing goodness, trying so hard to convince us of their profound religiousness or right-ness (and yet are still mean to one another), and when God is us, and we are God, and eternity is present right now, and when people transcend this idea of individual separation, then, it will be as it has always been: right now, peace on earth, love, kindness, truth, simply being to be. There will never again be the question, "To be or not to be," as that is what actually separates us.

And again in the paradox of language, in its inability to penetrate to the core of this thing, we are always being without being, moving without moving, seeing without seeing, here but over there and so on until it not only makes absolute sense but it doesn't need to make sense anymore.

And, yet, those who do not have it, have not actualized it, seem not able to get to it, are still stuck in the bucket. Perhaps in the back of some part of their minds they know It is there, or they get slivers of it, shards of rapture that fade as quickly as they come...what to do?

Be simple. Sit by a river. Sit. Quit trying. Logically realize there is nowhere to get to.

But action is still present. We want to act or not act because it is fun, actually we just enjoy the play of the play, the motions, the stillness, no conflict…. There is nowhere to go and we will have everything, and everything becomes interesting: the spider's web...the wrinkle in the wall paper...the sunlight shimmering on the water...the way the car rolls over a bump. It is all so very soothing like sitting fat in a warm bath, an eternal whirlpool; there is no more fear, no wanting, no getting something, and all is perfection in this perfect moment.

And if all this still does not at least point the way, then go sit for an hour, or two hours, in silence until the thoughts subside and until the world is you and then the peace of nature will signal you. And if this doesn't work, then get some kind of progressive therapy that might help. And then if this doesn't work, realize the key is inside, in your own potential. There is no outer force, no one who can tell you anything that will lift you up for long unless you internalize it, comprehend it, sense it.

Simply be. That is all. The rest is frantic running toward an illusory future or confined by some pattern of the dead, merry-go-round past. That is all. That is everything.

BE

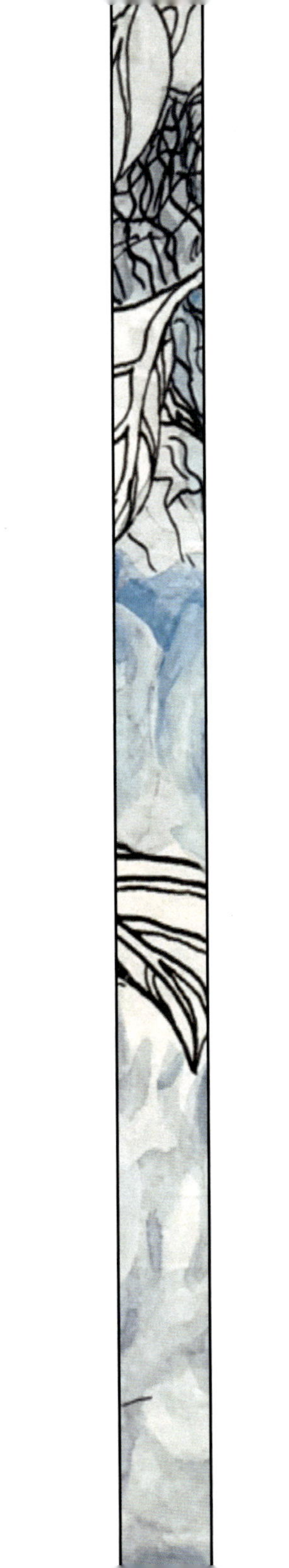

Chapter 8

Why Worry?

I would say most (if not almost all) worry, and if they don't, good for them. Worry is, again, trying to become anxious about the outcome when there is no outcome to worry about, at least not at this moment. So many live in this crazy state of being fretful of something that has not even happened, and then get themselves in a stir to become in a bigger stir until their thoughts take them into the world of worry.

The best advice when in or around this state is, as always: Exist now, believe in the NOW as eternal, and enjoy the ride.

My nine-year-old son and I went to the movies to play a video game that was in the lobby. It was at a 12-plex near our home, and it was a Friday night. There were so many people, and it was much too difficult for him to wait in line, fight or scuffle with other kids to play the one same game so we left. Then he asked me why is it that so many people want to go to the movies?

I basically said it is because they believe they need a distraction, need to do something that is more fun than what they are doing. Now I continued to tell him that I could sit in the car and have just as much fun as watching the movie going on in front of my eyes than actually following the droves of people into some dark place to be distracted.

He looked at me as if I was completely crazy, but when in the complete and utter state of inner peace, everything is interesting. The movie of people walking by, lights changing, the sound of the radio in the car...all of it is just like watching the best of any movie ever put out. In fact, it is a movie.

As the late great John Lennon said: "There are no problems, only solutions." And the solution is here and now and having fun being blissful, realizing each of us is eternal. There is nowhere to go, to get to, so why not stay here? Don't get flustered about what we have, or don't have, or think we need, or what society tells us we should do on a Friday night.

There is nothing to do and everything to do. It is the peace of knowing we are inside and outside and part of this foreverness. We will not die, we'll only view the world, and the viewing is all that is necessary to do, partake in, react to as we simply be.

But we have been conditioned to worry, to fear something in a future, maybe a calamity, to become tense about a present situation when there is no reason to become tense, or erratic or irritated or anything, for we are in a constant flow of love; that is all, that is everything.

So many people live in the timeline of getting somewhere, of how the 1970s were better that the '80s. And the '90s? My God, they were really horrible.

When we finally become, and when we finally understand there is only This, no That, then we have nothing but a smile for all those going somewhere, for those caught between games, those in transit to nowhere, absolutely certain they will get there very soon.

This is not paradox, not mumbo jumbo; it is as factual as factual has ever been, can be proven by being there, not by the separation of words, not by lengthy explanations, not by arguing with those who don't get it; but, we should at least attempt to explain it so as to point to, to leave markers, to seek out similar minds who get it, and who will smile because these words are so absolutely true. And, yet, so many see them as nonsense or voodoo or a game. It is not nonsense. These words point at truth.

Worry, and your life is fretted away. Worry, and the situational comedy becomes such a serious tragedy. Worry, and I bet you'll get some other poor soul to worry along with you, feed into your game, and then two worried people could start a worry congregation, a movement, and after a while, there can be a church where everyone worries, and all believe in the god of Worry, and it is just this absolutely absurd.

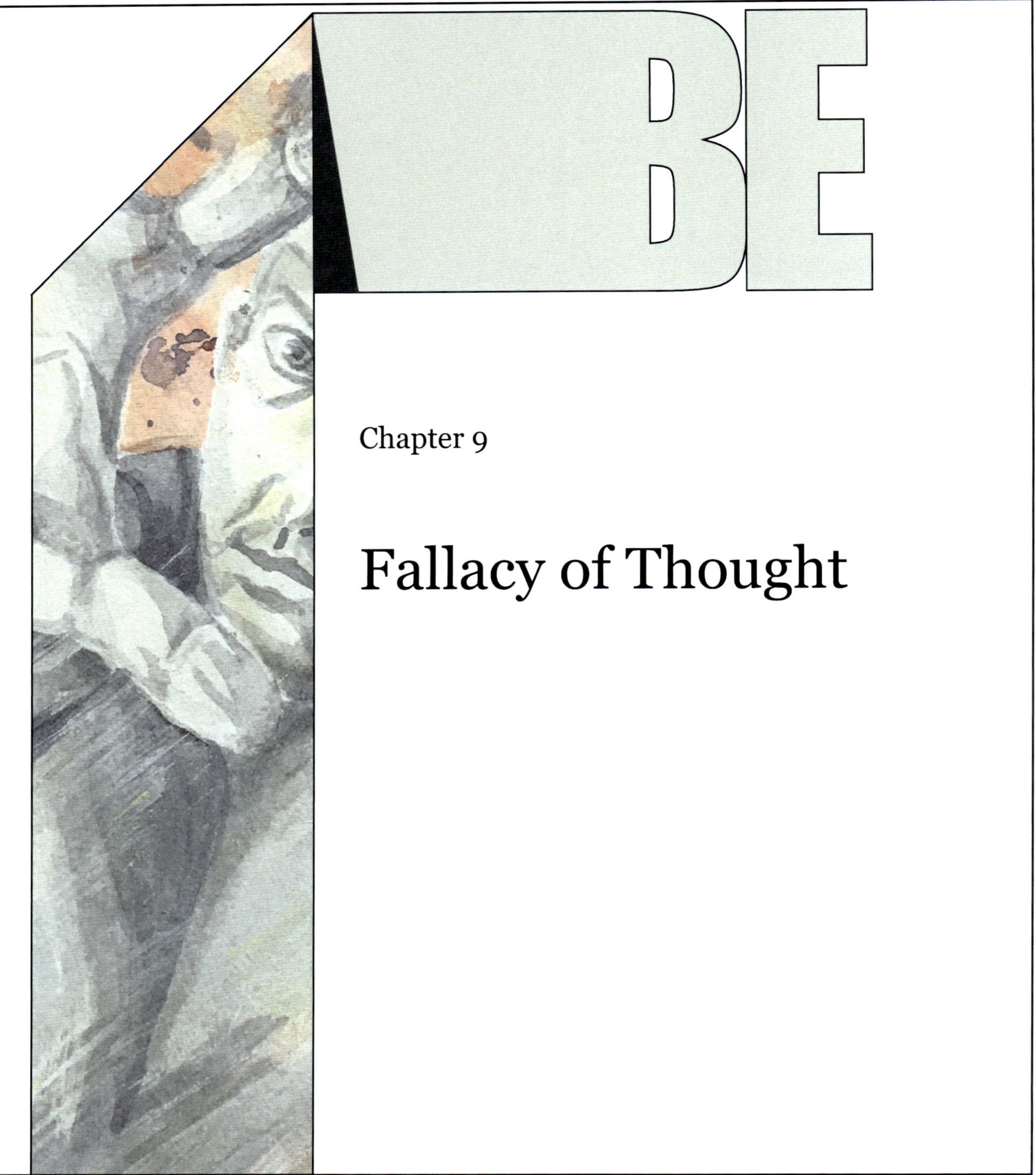

Chapter 9

Fallacy of Thought

I usually walk my dogs late, around 10:30 p.m. or so. It was a wondrous spring night, snow coming down and as I was sitting on the bench next to the school where the open fields are, and I realized, as the snow came gently down, filtered on me, gathering on my coat, my pants: I am snowing on myself.

This is not a thought, but a realization.

Thought is the prime suspect in this mystery, the "who done it" so to speak, the actual murderer who has killed God, killed the guests who were so very nice, then buried them all somewhere in a slippery, unconscious basement.

Thought is a tool to use, not a way to run us into the ground, into states of frenzy. As thoughts become our workers, as we control them and they control us very little, the awareness goes up, becomes heightened. We begin to see right through the illusion, understanding that it is the (our) thought process that, itself, causes separation, the fantasy world of imagination, of getting there, of planning, of worrying, a world where most love to go, to pretend, and stay like a good dog in a thunderstorm shivering, cold and afraid under the porch of their own deceptions.

It really isn't a matter of stopping the thoughts, more a matter of controlling, regulating, turning up the awareness. If we become aware of the music, the drama, see the world changing coats, chameleons on the march, if we see through the illusion of spinning fantasies about how we think the world certainly must be and, instead, just see it, and if we settle down and smile as the intricacies of 10,000 Things play hopscotch or other games, then the thoughts are not even present, don't have that separating feeling, factor, quality.

As I study Ken Wilber, the consciousness expert, and as I read his incredibly detailed explanation of the shadow, the ego, and pathological states so many are caught in, I realize I have little ground to stand on or training when it comes to psychoanalytical therapies, ways to merge self with self and so on.

But I'd say most do agree, as do all the masters, all the enlightening people who have written things, talked of these things, that it is back to God we desire to get to, back to this oneness.

Maybe I am a simpleton, but I believe all of us can get there without all this struggle, these intense and lengthy therapies, all the uprooting and digging up, all this examination and circumlocutionary whiplash, all the bashing of the mental demons that exist in our brains.

If we simply realize that our own thoughts are the biggest culprits, keeping us in states of fantasy, and then and thus simply get it, that we are living in the eternal, voila, all that we ever have envisioned, peeked at in moments of ecstasy, all come together to form the formless, to be the be-less, to capture a still-life bowl of fruit, being peeled before our very eyes.

Mine might be called the poetic approach to enlightenment, at least as it comes to the use of words to explain it, but It is all the same.

Control the thoughts, capture the illusion of thinking and tie it all down to the present and the present is, becomes, has always been, free to give us all we ever will ever need. We become the eternalness we have always believed was out there. It is not out there, it is right now, not over there, not a place of illusion to get to, not the Xanadu of great literature, no Utopia, but is actual, always, forever, right now. Simple enough?

Thinking is for the purpose of inventing, to recreate things, to have fun, not to promote depression, not to strangle the life out of a good poem, a good piece of rough road in the desolate parts of trying to get there.

Thoughts are our servants, will do our biddings if we guide them and understand them as limited, logical tools, as playful paradoxes scampering along the river's edge, the perception's edge, but they are our dogs, should be at our command, come back when we call, sit when we tell them (rolling over and playing dead really should be one of their best tricks). And then we can get on with the actual living stuff, the actual being stuff.

Dogs, all animals, they are complete and pure awareness. That is where we should stay and be happy. We can still feel compassion, and can still think when need be but only when the many see how absurd their "thinking" is, this pot of spoiled cabbage they remain in.

Thinking is the illusion that makes us believe the nonsense, the abstractions, the This and That which keeps us from true bliss, keeps us in mental states of believing we are right when we are merely playing with ourselves, a man wrestling with himself and can't seem to win.

So often we all are on some fantasy trip in our own minds, and the fantasy can go on forever until one fine and sweet day we get it: There is no place to go, no vacations to look forward to, no getting somewhere. It is right here, right now, the eternal play, the absolutely interesting world changing in front of our eyes, the highest drama of life happening in all directions from all pinpoints in one forever (and we should always remember), never ending...gush.

We need to tap into the gush and smile, for it is better than any movie, more grasping than the best novel, incredibly powerful, so very peaceful.

M. Dowling 6/18

It is the fallacy of thought that keeps us in our states of certainty, certain that we know what the hell is going on, the certainty of knowing that we can subdivide the universe into heaven and hell, into good and bad, into you and me, into all these parts that aren't parts at all. The parts are all of us exploring individual awareness, that is all.

We are cosmic awareness, and the only way to get to the highest levels of consciousness, where love is eternal, where bliss is a never ending reality, is to stop thinking about it — stop thinking about anything: We are there, here, where we should be, we just need to come to it, approach the divine and get in there and understand there really was, is, can never be a place to get to.

I guess the biggest question is why do we think? Why is it we love to entertain our intoxicating ideas — so drunk with our own interpretations? Why are we caught in beliefs that create separation? Why are we so absolutely certain that we have "mapped out" the way it is? It is impossible to figure out the way it is by thinking about it. Thoughts, in themselves, immediately create dualism, are mere representations, can only point to, allude to — never be the actuality of life.

Shut up (up there in the head of illusion) and the fantasy will fall out of the sky and we can be happy sipping tea on the veranda as the spring thunderstorms come rolling in. We can be happy scrubbing toilets. We can be happy laughing at the illusion going on in the heads of the ones who live in their certain little minds. Live in reality...not in the little mind. Live in the cosmic mind.

Again, all this may seem like words running off the back of ducks, may seem like a madman in his underwear preaching to designers of the day, may seem like absurdity with a half deck of cards, may seem like a long way from where we all need to get to. It is not. It is, as always, merely holding up the flower.

BE

Chapter 10

Poetic Interpretations

It is the sound of things, the motion of things, of the cars going by, the sky in the sky. Beauty is truth, and truth is enlightenment and peace on earth (and peace off earth) and peace inside.

What we seek is here, has already arrived: The cat in the backyard is crawling across the fence and becoming entertainment for us all to see, to be, to have and to — sort of — hold.

We seek the alarming beauty of this moment, the energy of This and That, being none of it but all of it.

Thoughts can be stopped by pure awareness: being aware of the chill of the air, the grinding of the tape in some old tape player, the feel of the carpet on the feet, the smell of something indefinable... somewhere, part of the air. Who knows, the changing of sunlight to cloud light and back to sunlight.

The stability in knowing is what we seek; knowing that we have it, that it cannot be lost, that they are It and we are It and whoever tags us is also It, and we play symbiotic games until we wish to play something new, until God is all of us, until we are not afraid anymore, to realize we, ourselves, can go into It. We are It. We can go wherever we wish to go because there is no place — to go.

And those who read this understand what? Words in a kind of nonsensical pattern? Perhaps they don't read something into the words, instead see the words (become the words) then perhaps they are getting close, they have arrived, they are there.

Invent no extra syllables. Find no underlying meaning. See through, and the "see through" is not a smiling paradox but a wondrous spit of ink, jet-blasted into the brain and back again all at once and the tendencies toward, to, into and out of, all become more absurd than these words themselves. So what do we do? What can any of us do?

One little suggestion. Laugh. Maybe not heinously, but heartily, like a sage after a long-table dinner and a good joke, like a poem inside a poem, lost in time and space yet still revolving. And maybe we could just sit and play finger games, touch the moment so languidly and deeply or shallowly, but touch it like a naked woman with boots, touch it like a gem in a tumbler, a crying child who got lost for a moment in some tizzy, touch it like a finger touching itself, an arm holding itself, a hug hugging everything, all at once, in one giant arm load. Isn't that what we all seek? To be and be and be and be and be and be until we, well...be?

It probably isn't to very many's benefit for a near-enlightened poet to string words together around the neck of something wonderful because interpretations get in the way. And he or they may find when looking at the art form with closed eyes, that they are lost in some imaginary world that crops up in the Mohawk part of a shaved-head night. They may even in some insipid format, believing this pseudo-sage has lost his sanity and is now weathered and leathered and mostly dementia sticking a finger in the socket of paradox as elves in the wee little forest...dance until they crack.

This is not true. Even the poet can be sullen and serious and quick to point out that, as absurd as it seems, as tenuous as it looks for someone outside the bottle peering into this world of enlightenment, it is not a glass-stained bottle holding distorted views, but more like a clear look into the heart of reality without being hung by the words...or something like that.

Go to the feet of the enlightened poets and praise them for their obliteration of the common perceptions and invite them to partake in a wine-and-dine dinner where they may speak their riddles and eat the pig's cheek meat...and burp.

What else is there, really? Somewhere to get to, some turbulent riddle to solve, some mathematical equation that could solve the puzzle of existence in one fell swoop?

We here at the enlightened institute think not, because, well, just because, and explanations would be to violate truth.

Do not violate truth, and it shall sit by your side like a clay pot, a tangerine ready to be eaten, a footstool, a sagacious fool...anything you want it to be.

Hear the tenderness of this world passing by, passing through, being the innards of something appropriate and beguiling, but absolutely certain.

Much like watching the icicle drip. That's it. A kind of thaw. It is nothing but, nothing less, nothing more, nothing but everything, merely yet exclusively, watching, hearing, feeling, sensing, being...the icicle's drip.

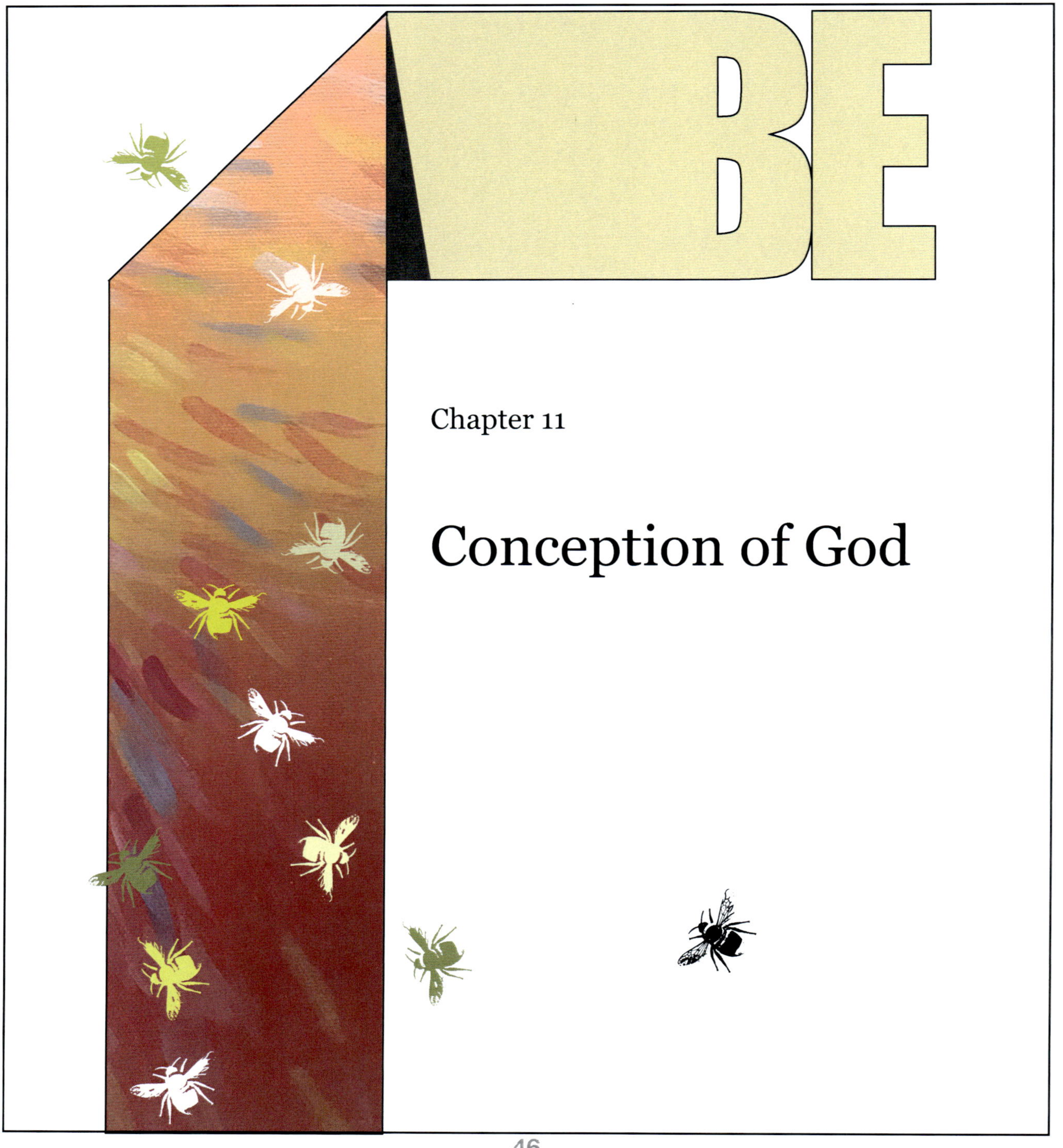

Chapter 11

Conception of God

Thinking of anything is the illusion, is the root of all separation, is what creates these worlds of some fatherly God in heaven, some omnipotent ruler who is outside from us, over there, out there, outside of what we call reality. This is not a divine or inspiring way to view God.

Kahlil Gibran said we should spend more time thinking about our relationships with each other (which we can understand), rather than all this thinking about God (which we cannot understand).

But we need to, at least, attempt to de-conceptualize God, get him out of the clouds, and find a reality amidst some kind of intellectualizing that then vanquishes the illusions we keep in our brains.

It is all tied together. There is nowhere to get to: This is God. Stopping the thoughts: This is God. We are part of everything: This is also God. We are beyond time and space: This is God. We are living in the ever-present eternal, a moment reaching out forever, the infinite: This is God.

There is no getting to, no seeing the tailcoats of God, for He, It, the Way, is always with us, in every breath we have ever taken. We ride in God. When we pray to God we are separating ourselves from God, for he is the prayer, doing the praying.

We cannot think about God because he is reality happening, and thinking is separating us from It.

So many sayings apply here: Let God. Trust in God. Find the Way, the Tao. It is all right here, right now, a burgeoning yet still life.

God is the fusion of all opposites coming together to form a timeless moment that we can be fully secure in, because, finally, at every level, we get it: There is no place to go, only a reminding of ourselves that this is It. No more vicious, thoughtful meandering, thrashing about in the mind to find something that is already with us, this us that is God.

We believe that it is much too brash, too conceited to actually believe that we are God. Instead, we might believe that maybe we're part God, maybe we were created by God, but to be God? Even the most egoed-out human is reticent to actually be God, but that is exactly what is happening here: We are all God. He is us, we are It and then there is no separation. There is no over there, no throne He sits upon, no finding him, no becoming close to our heavenly father.

Believing we are God or believing in our grandiose greatness isn't a lacking of humility. Rather, when we realize we are God, that God is everything, everywhere, all happening, right now, not someone to know when we die. He is not in some outer shell above the universe. When we see this stark but pervasive truth, then we become humbled. We become gentle. We see our deepest kindness. We settle into states of bliss beyond any conception and are at peace. And this peace is not an egoed-out version of being more than we really are, it is not our greatness getting in the way, it is simply very real, a realization that takes us over, that is thick, starch in the new shirt, a settledness of truth.

And truth is not thinking about truth. Truth is in the being, in shutting down the inner chatter, inner dialogue that is forever and so desperately trying to explain things, in the finding of answers that will never be there. To find is the mind playing games, keeping the fantasy alive.

Just try it: You are God. See It everywhere. Don't think about it and if you start thinking, command your mind to think more, and the thoughts will stop in an instant. And then watch. Be pure awareness. Know God in the trees, in the slight and warm breeze, in the sounds, in the illusion of destinations.

The world is our oyster because we are the world and the oysters. We are It trying, for some strange reason, so ardently, to be separate little doodads skipping away from our bliss. Don't do that.

All that is, is. All that isn't, is in our heads trying to find all that is. Such a game!

God is indefinable, is caught in a moment, not in an explanation. God is unending bliss, not some old man bestowing his wisdom on us from some heaven that we cannot penetrate until we take our last breath. We need to take our last breath right now, die right now so that we can live forever.

If we realize we are not a separate self, and yet we are God, then we grasp it, we lose our self into the Big Self, and that is frightening.

We want to be separate little unhappy entities, with a hope of a future that will never come. Once we banish this to fantasy, become God, then we begin to loosen the grip of the self and it wanders back home, into God, and we are pure and very heightened awareness. Thus, we treat all things with goodness and kindness because it is us, it is our very own self who we are dealing with, not other little separate selves, greedy little misers who want to get something, to get more.

We need to realize the illusion so we can find our peace, find real God-ness in every moment, find our reflections instead of being caught chasing rainbows, dreams that subdivide a future into a land of milk an' honey, a destination that we can never get to.

We are already in the land of milk and honey. We are already one with God. We are already merging with the All to become secure in the present, dying to find life, giving up the illusion so as to be fat and sassy in the eternal moment. We can share our acute awareness so that we see, be, are, find that if there is no place to go. Then we are everywhere all at once, and have become, have arrived. We are and always will be...that is plenty, always enough.

BE

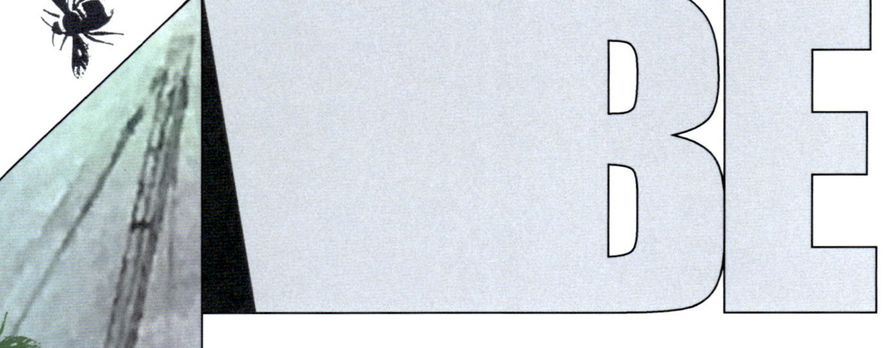

Chapter 12

Living in the Concrete

If thoughts and beliefs separate, then not thinking should unify. This is true to a point. We need to let thoughts happen, see them, see how they piggyback on other thoughts, how they can generate emotions that can create tension, or sometimes bliss. Yet, we need to see where these thoughts arise from and as we watch them, they will subside, leaving us in the absolute, a concreteness.

We must live in the concrete, see the sun coming up, watch the birds flying overhead, hear the chirping, smell the scent of jasmine in the summer evening air.

It is all so vivid, like a dream coming awake, when we realize there is no place to get to, the place we have always wanted to get to rushes up to us in the form of concrete images: the ticking of a clock, the music of the radio, the breeze, the stars hanging in the sky, being the sky.

And as so many of the sages have said: Once we stop even observing and actually feel, sense, become the world, once we are no longer just watching the world go by, instead, something inside of us senses, feels, realizes that we are the everything going by.

We are 10,000 Things that seem so separate but all are really us. Then you and me, we, it, they are all in a dance of becoming, a motion without movement. All is a swirl of the eternal coming and going, back and forth, here and there, confusion and clarity mixing well like high society, seamless poems that fit and never end and commence and stop.

When we realize we are the thoughts, the process, not just the stopping of the thoughts, but we are the movement, and we are the rain falling, and the sun, and our ancestry reaching out and holding us, setting us free, giving us the reasons to live, the meaningless reasons to live, then we arrive.

Living in the concrete is staying close to the present, watching it change colors, watching it salute the generals who are really the foot soldiers, who are beyond any absurdity that we can envision.

Living close to the concrete is being the concrete, is taking all our abstractions and accepting them but denying them, it is the last place to go. In fact, when there is no place to get to, no place to go, then we can go anywhere, do anything, release all fears into a small laugh...in a step toward.

When we do not seek to understand, our understanding rushes forth. When we do not wish for enlightenment, we have it come to us as a shy girl on a scamper. When we have given up the ship, the ship rises out of its own sinking illusion and flies us through the turbulent skies that seem now to be sweet, effervescent, complete.

Though words are like using a plastic bullet to kill an elephant, and words are mere shadows telling half-truths, we must at least attempt to say it: Live in the concrete. Beware of the detailed explanations of anything, and the anything becomes the everything. We aren't in hot pursuit; instead are in slow-go, in passive awareness that sees like a detached observer, yet everything we are observing is us actually observing ourselves. We are God and He is us and we no longer need to find out.

Freedom comes when we are not worried about freedom, when we understand in the center of our being rather than understanding with words.

Beware of the man with too many words, for he may paint a wonderful picture, but it surely will melt in the rain, in the sun, in the eternalness of this one and everlasting moment.

Live in the concrete: There is no other place to live. It is this solidness of life, its texture, the This and That which makes up the whole.

It is in our active participation that we energize the tools of our being and play the full gamut of our potential. And though there is no place to go, there is a potential seed of something growing, coming up, even if it is only a seemingly change of the eternal, a new coat, a new robe, a changeling, all is the process that goes in a circle. It is a circle of life and death, of coming and going, of one certainty that has its seeds in the present, in the concreteness of right now.

There is no other.

Peel away the layers of separatism until there are no layers left, merely a smile, a blissful acknowledgment of what used to be, the shell of what we used to see as the meat.

And the meat is in knowing we are in the concrete and we are not what we have conditioned ourselves to believe we are, but merely a certain kindness clothed in perception, love in the eternalness of this moment. What else can there really be? We are love in motion, finding out that we are all of it going by. We are the trees, the bees, the butterflies coming back to the cool air in spring, the insects crawling across a sun-drenched sidewalk, a dog sleeping in the back yard, a mind inside a mind, a hope without a future, a love riding the wind. We are the concrete; thus, it is so very easy to live here.

BE

Chapter 13

The Instant

So many think it must take them a lifetime, a library full of ideas, to get to their peace, to the conclusion.

The word satori is instant insight, a quick slash into the ultimate reality of all things, not after meticulous study, not after years of tortuous striving, not after middle age, after being with countless teachers, not something that we work toward, not something that we need to worry about, to fear like some future thing that may never happen.

Instant insight is all there is. When about on the daily routines, see it, be it, come to it, discover it on the radio, in the car, in the birds that are singing, in the ebb and flow of the this and that, and believe all of us are already completely enlightened. We are flooded with reality all the time, yet, somehow, in some human dysfunctionality, we have put filters over this reality that is always flooding us.

Take off the filters. Remove the blinders, but more than that, believe that everything you need, we need, they need, is with us: it's a friend, a kind of perfection we get to swim in. See the perfection, spread out into a cosmic consciousness where we are not the center anymore, we're not the focal point, only in a sensory kind of way, we are more like a molecule in a vastness, a cell in the body, a speck in the completeness, and even not a speck, more like a droplet that has found its way back to the ocean of cosmic consciousness. See the other people, other cars, the petty (sometimes poetic) dramas, feel the completeness of all things, the uniformity of life and motion and the burgeoning of all things from somewhere back to somewhere but actually not anywhere in particular.

These are not words of non sequitur nonsense that stab at a truth. And yet again, what else can mere words do but point to, say to the reader, over there is here. It is all an instantaneous flush, a simultaneous completeness becoming, being, staying, finding and losing.

Yet we have all that we need. We are enlightened beyond measure. We have this eternal swimming pool to swim in and can go underwater, catch the colorful fish, go fishing, sit at the edge of the shore of perception and understand there is no edge, no perception, no right or wrong, no dualism. And yet, we are still in the warm bath of bliss, of being there instead of getting there, and then all things are one thing, and God is us, and we are the answer by simply not asking anymore questions about existence, by simply (in an instant) getting there because we are already there.

So if there must be an exercise, do this: Believe in your complete peace. You and all of us are already in our inner peace, we already get it, we just need to watch our thoughts, notice where they come from, their point of departure, and own them. Watch as they take us to an anxious future that is illusionary, then simply smile. Watch as they create scenarios that usually never happen to disturb or disrupt our peace of mind. Peace is in the doing with a smile, in partaking of the situational comedy with love.

Once we use this supposedly newfound awareness to completely be at rest in the eternal, knowing we get to always be here because the image of the self is illusion, and the future is illusion, and the past is illusion, then we get to be forever in the eternalness of the moment. This is our womb where we can play, stay, reside, settle into a delightfulness of bliss and undulating security that cannot be gotten to with more money, secure jobs, more loved ones with us each step of the way, for we are the loved ones.

Thus, the exercise is to see, watch, try not to be the watcher but be that which is being watched, feel the centeredness of all things in some kind of flux, a motion, and in the pit of our consciousness, realize we are all this movement. We are the man walking on the sidewalk, the birds flocking together, the clouds zipping by overhead, the voice on the radio, the warmth of the cup of tea. And as we focus here, the instantaneous realizations will torch our consciousness. It will not end. It will become the universe happening rather than some petty, little entity trying to get what it wants so as to finally be happy.

Do what you think must be done and realize the enlightenment is the backdrop of all activity anyway...nowhere to get to, no machine to put on your head to drive you deeper and deeper into states of virtual consciousness. Then there is no sitting, no meditation as all moments are pure meditation with the awareness of a clear and insightful mind. There is only a purity of being.

The more we accept we are already at peace, the more we already know we are there. The sooner we think there is no answer to the puzzling questions of existence, then we are instantly at peace, instantly seeing through the illusion of worry, of depression, of having more, the illusion of tension and feeling so trapped, with no possibilities.

Each second is pregnant with possibility. Each moment is satori. Each moment we are swimming in a universe that is friendly, kind, soothing, and we are at peace, because there is nowhere to go, no over there, no sooner or later, no more "If only I do this, I will get this result." There is no more wondering, trying to figure out that which cannot be figured out — only by realizing it cannot be figured out, this produces the absolute answer that comes to us in complete clarity.

This instant is where we must remain to be in complete bliss. It is so simple that we make it difficult. It is so easy that we set up way too many rules to try to get to it. There is no getting to it, only seeing that it is with us right now, in a New York minute...that gets us to it.

Chapter 14

Truth

So many are looking for the truth, seeking truth, squinting to see through the misty confusion, the half-truths, the innuendoes, the sort-of-stuff and getting to the core. How can we get to the core, find meaning, see, be?

Truth is being. What else? If we are willing to be, to reside in peace, to become more and more kind, loving, caring, then this is the truth, there is no other. Lack of truth comes from the words we use trying to describe It.

"The truth of the situation is this: The truth is that he is psychotic, deranged. The truth is that she was abused as a child. It's Friday or Monday...this is the truth. The truth is that we need to make more profits in order to stay in business. The truth is that my wife and I love each other but I'm having an affair with a younger woman for merely sex. The truth is I did kill the butler when he was driving around in the master's limousine."

What kind of truths are these? Beauty is truth and truth is being. We need to look less for truth and more to being, settling into the universal consciousness, cosmic consciousness. So find the stitch between the "almost there" and "near enough," that moment in time when time melts, slips away like a bandit in the night, like a star setting beyond the surly sunrise.

When we expand our perceptions, find ways around our neurosis, get a grip, become, figure out how to live a day at a time, a moment at a time, then we find truth.

Truth is love, is giving, is being so completely in this one eternal moment that all action becomes appropriate. There is no systematic approach, no way of doing this or that. There is just a response to the drama, in a loving, sharing, kind way, for we can go this way or turn that way. There is no impatience. There is no getting something for ourselves, no agitation, no conflagration, no hopefulness or hopelessness, only a slur, a wave of motion, a feeling of complete oneness. This is truth.

Truth is not a separate little individual sentence that we can nail down, hammer it to a wall and signpost it up on some billboard that exclaims: "This is truth! Now you know."

Truth is in the existence, in the being, in the burgeoning of all things at once in one completeness.

If we are able, when we are able, as we see the illusion of the self evaporate (at least extend its boundaries, feel its connection to the whole), then we realize we are living in the infinite. And there is no rush at all because we have found eternity, right here, right now, not in some "out-there" heaven, no fear of an "under-there" hell. Then truth is not something definable in a sentence; it is not an axiom where upon we build a systematic set of rules and regulations. Truth is a sensation, an art of living, a smile, a gentle touch, the magic that surrounds the mystical as it walks through the fog of something wonderful. Truth is the bliss, the joy, the feeling of all things in a single blade of grass, the Buddha holding up the flower, the before and the after of making love in the bed of here and now, loving in the present, the This and the That, the 10,000 Things melting into a liquid state of primordial foreverness.

Beware of those who have the truth, speak as if they know the truth, for if someone says they know the truth and they try to put this truth into words, it immediately becomes fantasy, false, something we should be suspect of.

Truth is fluidity, flow, God-ness with us, beauty, a spring flower, a shy moment in the humble universe undulating. It is love, awareness, cosmic understanding, kindness, perspicaciousness, satori, meditation on this centered moment, basking in the eternal, finding blissfulness, erasing distinctions, healing the shattered parts into a whole — a healthy, living, caring, wondrous completeness.

The way to find truth is to find the true self, then the games, the situational comedies, the misled leaders, the entire world becomes naked, and we can see past the pettiness, the psychosis, the plots of the play. We then can see the drama going by as mostly actors being way too serious who need to be lightened up. Thus, we feel compassion for those in pain, those dying, those caught between the rock and the cliff, and yet we are still able to add our complete love and energy to it, heal the sick, the sick of mind, the sick of heart, heal with love and concern and peace. This is truth. Shouldn't it be enough?

BE

BE

Chapter 15

Truth of Fantasy

Some say truth is recognizable...true words are felt. Once I met a beautiful girl, and her truth was fairies. She told me she saw them everywhere...in the trees, six inches high, lovely little creatures, some that could fly, all magical and such. And she said she was mostly Native American, but that she had been a mermaid in a past life, said she had visions, and said these visions would come to her fast, sometimes slow, but would always be like premonitions. It was her truth. Who am I to deny her truth?

I met a young poet who said he was a pagan, said he made (with magic) $200 dollars materialize as he was trying to manifest only a dime for the bus that hadn't come yet. He said he'd overshot the amount a little, saw something just kind of flop over where he was staring in the parking lot...went over and it was $200.

Also, he told me he'd seen a cigarette light itself in someone's mouth, actually it just burst into flames before it could be lit, said he had also talked to giants and trolls...on and on the stories go.

I have a sister who sits in her room and gets visions from Jesus faster than spring lightning on the open plains, and says the holy spirit visits her, tells her the most amazing things, lifts her up to God. She actually has revelations, intuitive realizations, spiritual ecstasy — all at the foot of her bed.

And my own story: Once I walked down the river, the Colorado River, between Fruita, Colorado and Moab, Utah. It was an absolute nature experience. I was all alone, for ten days, in the heart of desolation, walking all day long with a backpack, then settling in at night and pulling out the sleeping bag as the night came quickly and the darkness covered the land.

One night I was sleeping by a very strange part of the river, the rocks looked like blood clots, kind of eerie. So I pulled up a lot of grass to make my bed right by the flowing sound of the meandering river.

I ate some prepackaged food, watched the light fade, nestled into my sleeping bag next to the quiet river.

As darkness settled, there was a giant splash in the water as if some gigantic boulder had fallen off a cliff and landed in the middle of the river. But there were no cliffs. I became terrified. I was full of fear. There was no phone to run to, no person who might help, no street lights to shed light upon the area. Nothing but stars and blackness. I was very alert, confused, trying desperately to put rationale into the rolling soup of reality.

Then it happened again. I jumped. I crawled near a bush and at that exact moment, I was attacked by something non-material, like electronic mosquitoes, buzzing all around me, not touching me but scaring the hell out of me, nothing I could do to explain the phenomena (even to this day) or fit it into the world of the rational.

I screamed, "What do you want?" and jumped out of my sleeping bag and ran to the top of the hill, way away from the river.

Finally, after many hours of pure-aware fright, I went to sleep without any other disruptions.

So what really happened to me? Was it water spirits, or something I conjured up, or an energy spot as Castaneda would talk of in his books with Don Juan? Was it truth, fantasy, or, as Ken Wilber says in his book Spectrum of Consciousness, this kind of experience that can only fit into part of the transpersonal band where all the mystical things can happen: astral projection, telepathy, gnarly gnomes, one-eyed Cyclopes stammering and sliding out of some storybook to convolute reality into a fishing hole of diabolical evil, of the mystical and arcane, a place where alchemists recreate reality?

One girl sees fairies in the city trees, as another young poet manifests money and talks with trolls, as I experienced things that have no classification — I'm sure so many have had experiences that transcend the day-to-day.

How in the world can we fit the world into a classification? It will not fit. Should I say to the girl concerning her visions that she is crazy, to the poet that he is psychotic? To the other pagan I once met who believed she had a black cat that was a spirit guide, had vivid dreams of having sexual fantasies unravel with this cat at night — what should I say to her? Who am I to deny these allegations of reality, ripples in the game of life?

When something doesn't fit, maybe we should extend the borders, erase the lines we have drawn, maybe we should keep the mystical in the sphere of possibilities, where fantasy and imagination commingle, where trolls bathe on the edge of castle moats, where the Loch Ness monster is as real as any business man in a suit going up an elevator lost in thought of how to make bigger profits.

When we accept the mystical as that...mystical, inexplicable, indefinable projections of reality onto reality (so as to confuse the best logicians) then maybe we can fly, reap the benefits of possibilities rather than conclude: This cannot be possible.

God, the universe, the inexplicable, the unrehearsed world of possibilities mating on the in-betweenness of certainty and perplexity, the undulating world of change, the possibility of eternalness that cannot transmute, will all stay fast in the arena of truth and God and Allness. So how in the world can we ever classify this crazy creation of God, this diversity of flowers in shades of red and gold, of every imaginable color? The wisps of clouds of such sincere white? Of chipmunks and squirrels chattering in the pines, where the elevation has always a chill in the sunny air? How can we ever fit the All into the files we have in our heads?

Ken Wilber has a systematic way of analyzing the consciousness, from the shadow, ego, biosocial band, existential, transpersonal bands to finally the infinite, eternal, Godhead, Mind (cosmic consciousness).

Ken Keyes calls it the different levels of security center, sensation center, power center, love center, cornucopia center, consciousness-awareness center, and, again, cosmic consciousness center.

Maslow had the hierarchy of needs, and so on...all may be right, all may be fitting a kind of reality into a workable plan.

But what if there is no plan? What if all the systems we are trying to lay over reality are merely our incessant ways of trying to capture God in a snapshot, put God in a bottle, like a firefly as it glows behind lucid glass? We are but trying to capture the essence of it all so we can explain it to our grandchildren who may or may not even care to listen. As we try to explain things, we lose the point.

From the Rubaiyat of Omar Khayyam:

For "Is" and "Is-not" though with Rule and Line, And "UP-AND-DOWN" with Logic I define,

Of all that one should care to fathom, I Was never deep in anything but—Wine.

Whether we like it or not, we are caught between things: illusion and reality, dualism, the This and That, the 10,000 Things of Lao Tzu. We are driven by rules and social convention, by hope of a heaven, by clasping a kind of certainty onto this supposedly eternal moment, grasping with closed hands at the uncertainty of each and every explanation. We are drawn toward myth and fantasy, toward the flame or sweetness of candy-coated dreams, maybe so as to rip us away for the ugliness of cancer, or from the crippled people, drawing us away from starving children, keeping us sane as some financial institution forecloses on our property.

Of all the unpleasant news we are forced to withstand, of all the pain and gut rot, so-called reality that seems so unfair (so unbelievably callused for a God of mercy to bestow upon his creation), of all the churning intricacies we find ourselves clinging to, psychic phenomenon, the psychotic homeless in the streets talking to those we cannot see, women dying in labor, children being born into abject poverty, millionaires who become neurotic and develop chronic fatigue syndrome...it doesn't matter the scenario. We are so desperately trying to figure this (something, anything) out, to somehow believe we have not lost all hope of understanding...the understanding any of it.

Some do not care. One young musician, seemingly a gentle soul, said, "I'm an apathetic agnostic. I don't know and I don't care."

Many young people don't seem to care.

Maybe they are healthier than those who have spent their lives, as myself, in the pursuit of something that can do nothing but elude us all. So many are in high pursuit for a fantasy to play, a game to invent, a fairy to see in the trees.

But as one last point of view of the fantasies we possibly self-create...a Zen story: A man promised his dying wife that he would never remarry after she died.

Then sometime after her death he did remarry, and each night he was visited by her ghost, and she haunted him.

After many sleepless nights, he went to a Zen monk, and told him of his dilemma.

And so the Zen monk asked the man, "Is it true, then, that your wife knows all now?"

"Oh yes," said the tormented man. "She is now of the all-knowing."

So the Zen monk told the man to take to bed with him a sack of beans. And instructed him, whereupon when the woman would appear, to hold out a clenched handful of beans to his ghost/wife and then ask her how many beans were in his hand.

And so that night, the man did as the Zen master said. And when his nightly visit came and his deceased wife appeared to torment him, he held up a handful of beans and asked her how many beans were in his hand, whereupon the vision disappeared, never to torment him again.

I guess we should, at least, say: Beware of any fantasies we get caught in.

The problem with most fantasies is we like that they torment us, the way they torment us: our sexual fantasies, our believing in cute fairies, our hopefulness of a future of getting rich, famous, somewhere rather that where we are at. We must kill our fantasies so that we can get eternal life, so we can fully enjoy the realness of what is, swim in the eternal moment. Let go of that which allures us, no matter how illustrious, how iridescent, how enamored we are with our fantasies...a small price to pay, I'd say, to finally find what we have always been looking for: peace, tranquility, inner contentment.

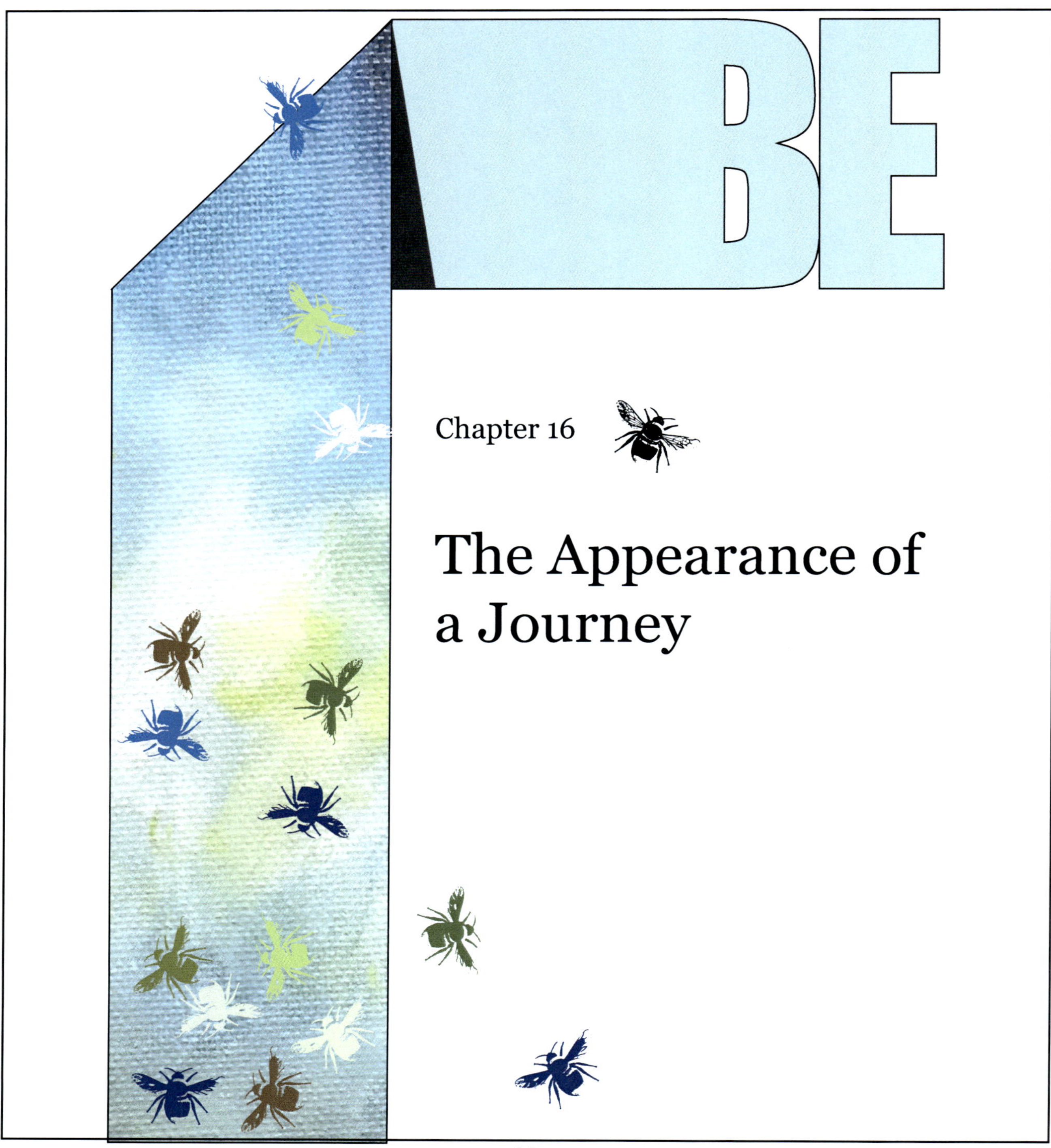

Chapter 16

The Appearance of a Journey

Many will debate this eternal moment of the NOW, a moment that has no roots in a past, no addiction to a future, many will say our bodies age, this is what is real, our time elapses, we evolve, and are in some kind of state of motion, a journey.

Some, it seems, are so addicted to this future that they sacrifice all peace and contentment to try to have it, get to it. And even if they do achieve this futuristic world, get the perfect retirement plan, the house near the beach, the perfect world that they have sought, can they now, as it is in their laps, enjoy it? Or is it that they have conditioned themselves to look so hard, so desperately and intently toward a future, that when the future they envisioned arrives, they have so conditioned themselves to keep going, toward another future? Or they become sullen and surly as their frantic search of a perfect future has robbed them of their ability to enjoy the present.

However it can be debated, looked at, analyzed, we are on some kind of journey, maybe a pleasant pressing toward higher consciousness, or a movement in time and space, a kind of personal evolution and growth, where we grow in degrees, wisdom comes in spoonfuls, and eventually in the way of a kind of appearance, time becomes a friend, not merely an illusion, but a slipping off of skins, of fantasies, a way to smile as we see the flux...flex.

And of the greatest sages and teachers of the world, all have pinpointed happiness, or joy, or universal bliss to be a moment in our perception of time that cannot be discarded, or lost, this moment that is, in appearance, forever changing but has the guise of something absolutely eternal sewn into its seemingly to and fro movement.

So many want to regret the journey, keep to the safe roads, so afraid to rock the boat, to lose too much, to risk too much because, well, they would have to start over again, rebuild. But if life is a journey, and it, in all appearances, seems just that, should we not take it as mostly adventure, dream up the impossible, dream up the incredulous and press toward it with a smile rather than with a clot of fear in the throat? Should we not feel the nuances of the cool stream, the hot whirlpool, the soft breeze rather than sit behind a television, or work so hard that we are extruded human tissue shoved through a social ideology that pushes us on to have and to hold something, anything they, the social order, has taught us to strive for?

And as Rudyard Kipling wrote in his poem, “If”: “If you can dream — and not make dreams your master,” then perhaps we can have it all, dream but never believe it’s our dreams that will give us our salvation. It seems that being blissful in the moment, enjoying the process...this is the answer to the riddle of existence.

Yet, maybe we must have something to always look forward to, even if we are in the eternal present...as if keeping the game alive.

I once had an inspiring professor in college. His favorite subject to teach in his philosophy class was Zen, and he would deliver the lecture standing on his desk. He would say, "Always have something to look forward to, even if it is your next meal."

Of course, there is some truth to this, though all we ever need is in the quivering pinnacle of the NOW moment, we still need to somehow become excited about a place to go, a meal to eat, a new way to approach this fantasy journey.

I see reasons why we can fully live in the present moment and still look toward something in, what so many call, an illusory future. Some call it hope. Some call it faith. Some call it a Friday night out with shots of tequila and friends, waiting in the eaves as Thursday afternoon comes falling down.

Ken Keyes wrote that if we are caught up in desire, emotional addictions of having to have what we think we must have, then we are definitely living in a fantasy, chained by our emotional patterned responses to that fantasy. If we need to make hundreds of dollars or they will take our car away, and it seems a life and death situation in our own minds, and we do not achieve this, then we become depressed because we have fallen short of what we really have conditioned ourselves to believe that we must have in order to be peaceful, content with the here and now. Obviously, we thus become frantic, and suffer. It is not the situations or circumstances that create this suffering. It is simply our way, the way we have conditioned ourselves, to respond to circumstances that will trigger our same patterned reactions. Thus, we see few options and may not believe in the value of adversity. Why not define crisis as: "Opportunity riding the dangerous wind"...as an old Chinese proverb would put it. Instead, if we prefer to make the money we need, then we will not be disturbed if we only make $100 or nothing or five bucks as we are not emotionally involved in the result and the outcome.

Commonsense must make us realize, that, of course, there is an absolute, an eternalness and realistically, we can ride the present in order to be completely blissful. But we also must function in the world as we are surrounded by situations that can make us react, can actually make us create dis-ease.

Say, for example, the IRS takes $2,000 out of my checking account without even telling me because of back taxes I haven't paid due to an IRA early withdrawal penalty (this did happen to me). And say that $2,000 is needed to pay for food, a car payment, a mortgage and things like that, then can we merely drift through that specific moment as if it is any other moment and gently pick up the phone and beg the IRS to please give us our money back and then go on our merry way without some strife, some emotional reactions?

Ideally, the greatest of the sages could probably do it, let it go, go live in a cave, eat berries, realize all things work out, be so calm and find solutions in this innate placidness. But we are riddled daily with situations like these so that we must become of higher awareness to deal with them, so as not to go over the proverbial deep end and, instead, smile as if it is a drama and we are lightly playing a part, a minor role in the giant production. We need to see through the illusion of needing more and more money, of needing more and more of so many things so as to capture a future that will promise happiness. Instead, we need to trust that the universe will take care of us, and it really is an actuality that we can get all we need from this incredible, one single forever moment. It is simple in theory.

Ken Keyes, in his book Handbook to Higher Consciousness, tells a Zen story: There was a man fearing for his life as he was being chased by a tiger, and it was chasing him to the edge of a cliff. As he got to the edge of the cliff he noticed there was a vine for him to climb down, and he did just that. But looking below him he saw more tigers waiting at the bottom of the cliff for him. And just above his grasp was a mouse eating away at the vine, about to gnaw through it. At that instant he noticed a red, fat, ripe strawberry on the side of the cliff right next to him. So he plucked it off the vine, and it was the best and sweetest strawberry he'd ever tasted.

And so we are always being chased by tigers, but there are plenty of strawberries to enjoy. So if we focus on the strawberry (the present) and let the tigers of the future and of the past (even the ones that seem to be in our present) only get us when they get us, then we can live blissfully, and many times these tigers will evaporate before our eyes as we focus on the strawberries...and often these tigers are not even there, only in our minds, our fear of some disastrous future that seldom happens.

Some believe if we reside in the eternal present, sit fat and happy in this completely satisfying moment, then we have no motivation to do, to get, to become, to even take care of the simple necessities of life, like eating, cleaning the house, brushing the dogs, making a living for our families.

This is totally false. It really is this simple: When hungry, eat. When tired, sleep. When in need of money, make it. When driving down the road to work, drive down the road to work. When planning, plan, but realize it is an illusion as we are just using our thoughts and our logic to do what (in our mind) we think must be done, doesn't in anyway make us lose our awareness to enjoy the journey, to feel the completeness of the moment.

Do what must be done. The IRS takes your money, find a way to get it back. The car runs out of gas, get a gas can full of gas and pour it in. When dinner is served, eat it. When the dishes need to be washed, wash them.

Though we are eternally happy in the present, we are still in this illusionary world and must live, have responsibilities, may need to shine our shoes, take the children to school, shop at the grocery store, mow the lawn. There is nothing that says how we must do things, but we certainly must do them. And it seems a much better perception to actually want to be responsible, actually want to love and serve and give to our families, actually want to plan out a future just to see if we can self-create this malleable reality of things and direct the illusionary dramas we are caught in, or that we find ourselves pleasantly playing. It's okay.

The illusion, suffering, pain, agitation, the pathologies come when we must have this illusionary future, when we see opposites and dualism, and this future we desire won't do what we say, or when we are frightful of things that probably will never happen, or why we worry about them before they happen.

I'm sure we have all heard that, "A coward dies a thousands deaths, a brave man but one."

So we are fully filled by this incredibly wondrous moment, can touch upon the eternalness of it if we simply slip away from the past and the concept of a future we must someday possess. But we can also use this present moment to plant seeds, to organize, to do what in our minds we think we should be doing. Action and non-action are the same thing.

No matter how eternal we are, how innately or intimately we realize it, no matter if we understand there is really no place to get to, no future event that can bring us peace, no one thing out there that will bring us our truth and yet we still can work toward a life of experience, of wanting to stretch our routines and drink with beautiful women, eat new foods, taste the pleasures of life...as long as we don't need these pleasures, as long as we see through the illusion and are willing to still be of the illusion, "in this world but not of this world" so to say, then we can live peacefully in this world.

Life is an absolute eternal moment, going over it and over it until we get it. But life is a bagful of many experiences that have emotional value, impact that can free us, or torment us, a series of appearances that we can either deny or believe in so strongly that we miss the eternalness of this perfect moment.

We are actors in a play of some made-up eternal dance, so if we are still alive, breathing, then should we not act as if it is real, act as if we are great actors and take the benefits from our acting careers?

The journey will always appear to be a journey, and we will stumble upon revelations, we will find our peace, we will serve others of our world, we will grow in wisdom, we will alleviate the dualism of here and there, of life and death, of coming and going, of real and fantasy, of true and false, and eventually, in fact at this instant, be, and be some more, and enjoy the iced tea, and feel the wind in the alleys, and sense the beauty expressing itself.

We were, also, created to express ourselves, not to just sit and become one with God. And it is in our expressing this that we can feel our God-ness, that we can whisper secrets in the ears of mermaids so that we can fit into our niche between time and the eternalness, between cosmic consciousness and maybe not complete cosmic consciousness quite yet, only because we prefer it that way.

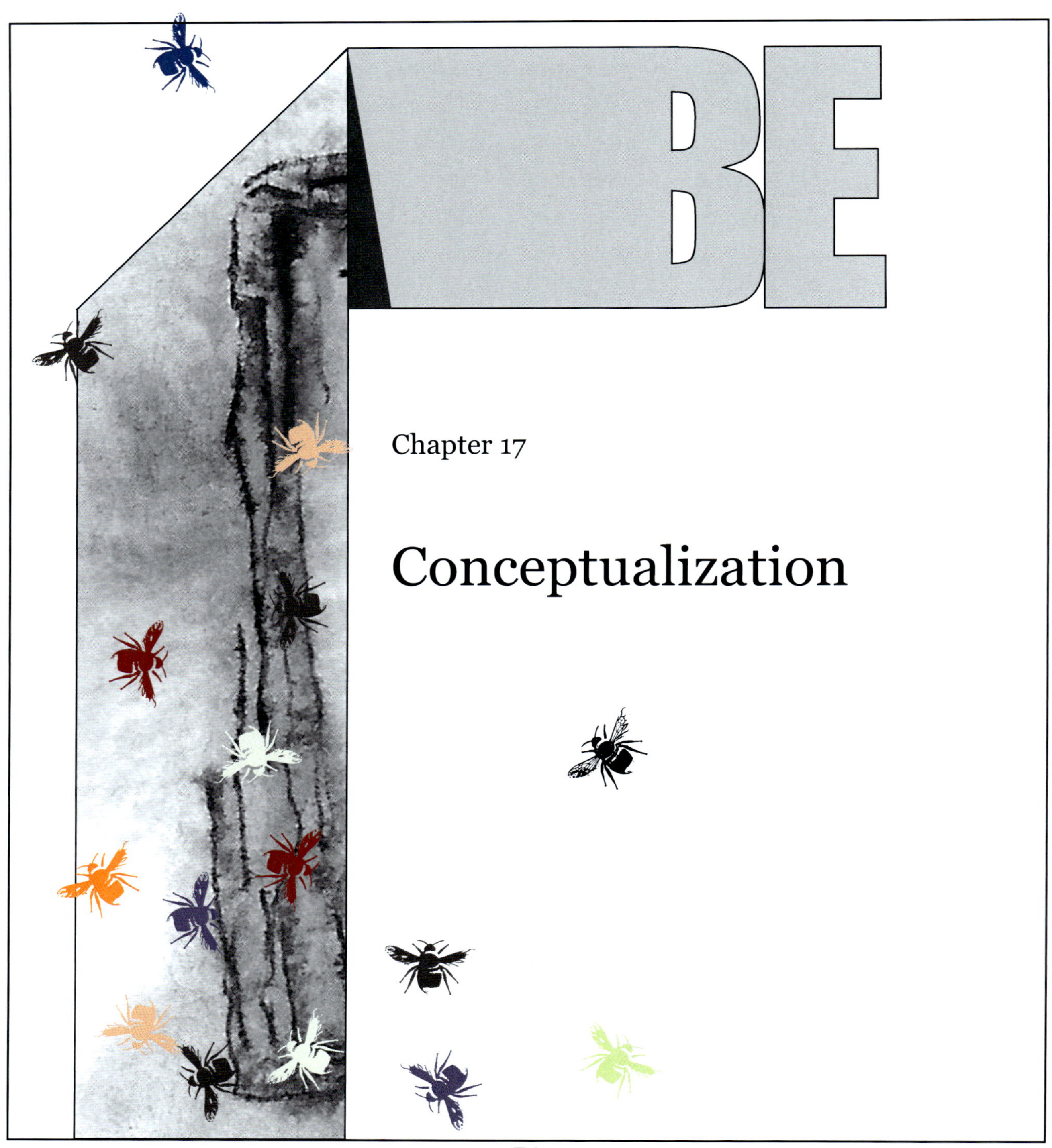

Chapter 17

Conceptualization

It seems we have been trained (or it's in our makeup), to have some kind of desire to figure things out, from the death of James Dean, to the patterns of ice on Neptune, from building religions, to building superhighways, to figuring out what is romantic love, to understanding the tiniest particle, seeing how small we can get — or get to.

We need (or think we need) structure. We need to corral all things into some kind of meaning. And the human mind is good at this, can take any situation: a divorce, the outburst of a child, the reason a certain program on TV is on a certain night at a certain time. We so intently engage in the mode of conceptualizing.

Why is it that we do this? Why is it that we need to put structure to all things, be it mystical experiences, to why our astrology charts are so very accurate these days?

We just need to know, to have certainty that we know, know that the laws of universe are real and static, and the supramundane is a castle in the air, mermaid capitols in the Indian Ocean. But most of our conceptualization is not mere fantasy, is more accepted, like building a house to live in, similar to the other track homes, the subdivisions next to us, just slight modifications so our neighbors don't get mad.

Seems most people are convinced by the culture or slightly adlibbing their way through so-called reality, like the man who works for a giant corporation, learns to manage people as he was taught, but surely develops a style that is his own, similar but idiosyncratic. Or the woman who believes in the Catholic religion, believes in heaven and hell but has to twist a few of the concepts, tweak them a little, so as to help mild sinners someday get to this proverbial heaven.

We have theories about everything: why we exist, why animals should or shouldn't be used in medical research, why a googol is a drape to throw over massive understandings of numbers...and it goes on and on until the day we expire, throw down our machinations and wander into the All-ness. But we don't need to wait that long.

Part of getting to our peace, rapture, bliss, state of and shades of enlightenment, is giving up on our theories, by simply not thinking, as this can directly get us in contact with what is, without all the conceptualizing, as we watch our minds try so incessantly to categorize, to figure out, to classify, to theorize, to add fences to places where we need to keep the cattle from straying.

So as we approach each day, we need to watch from where these theories arise, as some are gurgling up from areas where we have pain. And if we let them, we can weave entire scenarios and facades of how the world of "what is" should be. And we need to watch the place these thoughts come from to spin our golden fantasies, inspiring little bits and short-sighted visions of what could be. Thus, as we watch our daily thoughts, as we witness them, not judging these thoughts, not clinging to them as truth, yet seeing them as mirages in a self-professed desert trying to create a heaven, a fantasy, trying so hard to find a place for us to drink, to sit a spell and think and spin more delusions, then our thoughts become ghosts, phantoms, pleasant reminders that they are simply the churnings of the mind, nothing else, and all is okay.

And as soon as we do not take our theorizing too seriously, but merely as the way of the mind, as an ebb and flow of who we are, and let these thoughts pass through the brain undisturbed, without clinging to them as fact or fiction, then we can feel the present so deeply, ride the wave of time and can blissfully realize we are at home everywhere we go, and all things are us and there are no theories that fit, for they are, were, have been a simple stab into the darkness to find a reason.

Reasons will not make us happy. Ideas can only hinder us. Concepts will only put layers on reality. Thinking is our way of establishing order where there seems to be none, finding truth in an idea where there is none. It is simply our desire to unmask that which is, by stripping away its clothes — although this cannot be done with thought, ideas, concepts, reasons, analyzation or classification.

This is not a new approach, but it is so valuable to keep aware so as to let the fences go down, to make the open plains, again, open plains instead of plots of land, instead of subdivisions.

If we quit subdividing reality, then reality becomes a wholeness, we become an energy source, we become all things instead of running from being all things. Thus, we are unified, swimming in the eternal, and all the thoughts and classification that we impress upon our world becomes abstract nonsense that is for one purpose: a game to play; something to do when we don't want to be; a reassurance that things are and must be how we think of them; all but an intellectual masturbation of trying to get to a mental orgasm. It just doesn't work in our favor.

Chapter 18

The Magical Shift

If everything so far that we have said is true, if there is no place to get to, if we are eternal beings, pure energy changing forms, part and parcel of God, if we are already enlightened, then we just need our awareness to catch up.

So if we are always blissful anyway and the only thing that creates suffering is our own misconception of getting something, somewhere, getting more, being drawn toward an illusionary future, if we are completely in the process of the ever-changing world and we are not just looking at the change but we are the change...then all these things are what frees the magic, aligns the parts, helps us make a slight shift in perception that gives us all that we could ever need and want.

Isn't it true our freedom comes from realizing that we don't know, can never know, and that our freedom comes from realizing we are eternal fish swimming in the eternal sea, in the forever river of time (though we seem to be going upstream at times). We cannot have certainty because certainty implies we are above it all, have found the answers when the questions were stilted, asked in the wrong way in the first place. We so much want to entertain fantasies of God did this to me, or all of the sudden there was this situation that just manifested itself. And intuitively these things are so very possible, but how they come about, why, how the magical man had everything fall into his lap and was sitting atop of a million dollars that a complete stranger left him, or how the two lovers met on some poignant edge of a Friday night in unrehearsed bliss and fell instantly in love, or how the government sent that man a refund for $10,000 that wasn't even his, or how the elderly man won the lottery...all these seemingly predestined factors, all these perplexities, we will never be able to define, put a finger on. And yet, whether the drama gets thick or thin, whether we find gold or mold is not nearly as important as looking and seeing and being.

When we are here and realize the getting to somewhere is the illusion, that the frustration of the moment is seeded in wanting a result of a future that isn't happening, isn't going to happen, when we feel part of the process, understand without thinking about it that we are the actual process, understand and actually sense our eternalness, when we can walk all the azure edges of perplexity and knowing yet care not (and enjoy it), when we can describe nothing and ascribe to all things, when we are blissful because of the motion and pattern of life, and we feel, know, sense, realize, have united with all things, see ourselves as the magic, the mystery, then we finally get it. Then we are the cloudy days, the shift in the haze, we are the slow jazz, the bells chiming in the steeple, the birds singing. We are the snow falling. We are the happenings happening, the fantasies, the illusion, the see-through parts, the God of

Gods. We are being fed incorrect information and we don't care. We see the truth and smile, we are leftover bits of the absolute before it was chopped up by Aristotle, before anyone cared what the highest prime number could be, before we divvied up life into separate religions, ways of thinking, before the masks were put on and put on and put on until the many were the many confounded, the few became the few against another many enemy.

The magical shift is to be, to see ourselves in the sunny day, in the snowy afternoon, to be the child playing, to be the birds chirping on the window sill, to feel the motion of all things, to understand not with logic, not with some devised intellectual harangue, but to understand that we are, all is, and really (in the gut) we finally get it that the blissfulness of living is as real as keeping it in the shirt pocket, much like a swig or swill of good whiskey. And, thus, we take that step beyond any words, beyond any explanation into the magical shift, the free ride, the ultimate center of all things where words exist as play things, where beauty exists as reality, where the gurgling up of the burgeoning moment is but the keys typed out on the computer. A state where the sounds, the events, the turmoil, the reasons cease to exist and we begin to heartily take on the universe because it is us. We are it. And all things that create in us any discord are merely us, ourselves trying to get more for the us which is already giving us all that we need. Simple enough?

The magical shift can come anytime we want it to and it can run away anytime we wish to perceive a new illusion, get lost in a new or old routined illusion, play new word games, become too serious of this situational circumstance that is only tragic in its perception, only evil in its contrast to what we envision to be good. And if we step into the circumstance, go to the watering hole, drink from the eternalness of God who is with us, who is holding us up to the light, who is giving us all that we need this very instant, then we swim away like tadpoles in a new primordial soup. We rush to the waterfall and stand under it and become the water falling on our naked bodies. We give room for the universe to come and go, to play its sultry music or piercing silence. We give the universe leeway. And we, ourselves, become the leeway, the freedom that is sprouting up all around us like daisies in the rock garden, like jewels in the desert, like all things doubling back on themselves until we are the doubling back, until we are the shifts, we are the perfection, the non-dual, non-separate entities of one entity, and we are safe to fly to New York or quit our jobs or stay in our jobs or travel Asia, or travel the backyard to admire a shy flower near the storm drain.

It really matters so little as we make, capture, sense, become the magical shift.

And it is not a poetic shift, nor a non-sensical shift, as we would love to believe, nor a place only the creative go to bury ancestorial bones, bury their sorrow, is not a place of castles in the sky and wonder why, nor a place of children's storybooks, of ogres chasing the fire-breathing dragons into some boiling ocean of imagination.

It is. The magical shift simply is. We are already it. It is with us like a guardian angel, like a friend, an answer to every question that could ever be conceived of being asked, like a wholeness that unifies us and brings the so-longed-for harmony.

Try the magical shift, for even if you do not try it, as even the word "try" implies trying to get somewhere, it will try you. It will find you, like a shy deer coming up to the still man in the quiet meadow holding some fresh picked grass.

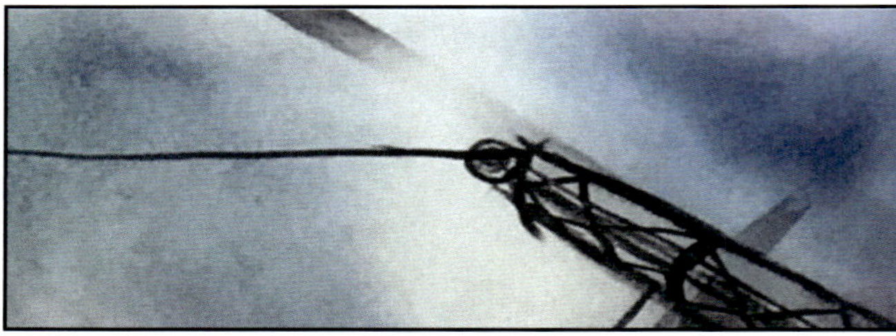

Chapter 19

Being Peaceful in an (Un)Peaceful World

So many want to blame their unhappiness, their suffering, on the outside world. Common things to hear today are that the planet is completely screwed up, and that we live in horrible times of pollution, war, crime, and so on.

So many base their peace on an outer unrest. If the world is in turmoil, if the murder rate is on the rise, crime in the inner cities is up, drugs are being used and abused by the youth, and so on, then they have a right to be unstable, unhappy, at risk.

Tara Singh in a little talk he recorded explained about this place in Africa where French and German people were living (actually a movie), without outside news, and they enjoyed each other's company because they were European, celebrated the same holidays, drank wine at dinner, and so on. Then one day a newspaper came and informed them that their countries were at war...actually, it was the beginning of World War I. After the news, the French and the Germans began not to get along. Although they were far away from the strife, far away from the circumstance of a war "out there," they eventually wouldn't even talk to each other, and even six months or a year after the war had ended, they were still playing the hate and I-don[1]t-like-you game because they hadn't received a newspaper telling them that the war was over, that the situation was now okay and they could be friends again. But, because of circumstance, because of thinking the outer world was tied to their happiness, in their minds they created a separatism between themselves.

How often do we do the same, fill our minds with the news, feed on the negatives of what sells, then become abashed and astonished about the horrid things happening in all parts of the so-called civilized world.

The media, in its present breadth, in its global reach, has brought mankind together only to separate us even more, to create more illusion: global concern, uneasiness, a reason to get all upset, to justify why we should feel so upset.

My great-grandmother, would always say: "The world isn't like it used to be, too many bad things, too many."

When she was born in 1890, there wasn't the inter-connectiveness of the media, the notifying us of the starving people in Africa, of the wars in Somalia or Bosnia, of the nightly horrendous murders happening daily in almost every major city in the U.S.

And when my grandmother was being raised, you picked the corn, killed the pigs and chickens yourself, talked with friends down the dirt road, walked down to the little grocery and talk some more some more about the weather, a little gossip here and there. Back then they weren't bombarded with all the tragedies that were happening daily all over the entire earth and then made to sit in front of the television to exclaim, "Hey, it is true! The world is really screwed up and getting worse and worse all the time."

Years ago it wasn't so much in your face, but now, we as compassionate beings get involved, concerned, worried, frightened, even if it is on a subconscious level.

Two hundred and some years ago, even Thomas Jefferson said, "As soon as I stopped reading the newspapers and started reading only good literature, I was much happier."

If we fill our perceptions of the world with murder stories, hurricanes, tornadoes and starvation and whatever else the media needs to fill us up with all this tragedy to make their ratings better, then we get the illusion that all our happiness, all our bliss, depends on the state of the present economy, the crime rate in our state, in the state of New York...even the weather outside can change our attitudes, seems so ridiculous, doesn't it?

Peace is inside, or outside, or is at least with our perceptions. Guess what? There is not a place to get to.

It all comes back to the same thing: We are happy if we realize we are basking in the eternal. The past does not confine us. The future cannot scare us because they are both impostors that manipulate mankind to be agitated about a future or stuck in some illusionary past.

So when we know (and not merely intellectually) that all our bliss and radiance come from residing in the present, that all else is illusion pushing us and pulling us, making us frustrated about things we have no need for, no right to even be frustrated about...then we get it, become It.

Sure, crime exists. Sure, starvation is a sick human problem that needs to be solved. But all the outer turmoil cannot and should not create inner turmoil. We shouldn't let circumstance wedge separatism between us and them because there is no "us and them," only us, only one world in motion, only a gurgling-up of reality, only a placid moment being a placid moment being a placid moment. It is in our trying to run away from this placid moment, our trying to get somewhere else, trying to feel we are failures because we were failures last month according to society's rule, that this potentiality of the present is suffocated, strangled. And we end up existing in some wavering thought process of reality, groping toward a future that never arrives and clinging to memories about a past of which we only have slivers and (usually misrepresented) pieces.

M. DOWLING 6/18

Outer circumstance can have an effect — it can be in our face, like a car accident happening in slow motion that we may be part of. But only when in an accident, be concerned. If watching the accident, be empathetic and compassionate. Do not condemn the world because you feel upset. Do not judge the entire planet from your depressed state watching the news on your couch, blaming the entire world for your situation in it. And it can be more subtle than this as we are motivated by what we are convinced is important, merely adding to the problem, being convinced that having a new car is freedom.

The beauty of God is that he gave all humans the ability, whether rich or poor, whether intelligent or dull, whether old or young, of any and all races, the absolute ability to be peaceful in this moment. We have been pre-programmed inside to be blissful no matter what, no matter if there is war in Iraq, whether we lose our job or are making a million dollars a month. All we need to do is to realize that we have been deluded by convention and the social convention we partake in propagates the illusion of misery and strife so as to make it appear real. So many love a good illusion and have seldom (if ever) tasted or experienced eternity. So few (and so seldomly) have seen the sunset and the full moon rise over a misty pond in the seam between spring and summer. And yet so many believe these are mere moments of bliss that cannot be sustained, so why try? And they run back into their worlds of illusion where all the other people verify this illusion with their convinced conventions of how things really are.

Few have the inner strength to go against the convention and see the naked truth, so afraid to step away from the common perceptions that are so ingrained, and instead, get to the oneness of God, the world, the neighborhood, the oneness of being.

Circumstance is the illusion we slip into because, well, we always have before. Slip away from the circumstance into the peace of each moment, and let not the (un)peaceful appearances create any kind of illusion that we live in a screwed up world so we also should be/feel screwed up, be the victims, mere half-crushed and sinking ships on the turbulent sea of uncertainty, always in crisis or near crisis, always ready to go under, always running frantically away from something that is chasing us...be it death, poverty — any insecurity.

This is not so. There is nothing chasing us, not even death. We are happy to the point of understanding that circumstance is illusion, bliss is real, truth is long-lasting and you, me, we, they, us, are of the same mud, come from the same source, are the same source. There is no reason to fear, to run, to hate, to fret, to feel we must manipulate and delegate and get things from each other.

Help, love, give, feel the undulating bliss, be, and all the world will mend itself in a flash, all illusion will unfold like a good book magically opened to the best part of the plot, to the climax, opened to this exact instant that is and has always been the climax.

Chapter 20

Right Action

The Buddha talked of right action. What can be right action, right behavior, right perceptions, as Lincoln would speak of, "rightness?"

What are values that we should maintain, believe in, realize?

What is correct knowledge?

If we live in the present, do not abstract into theories, ideas, ideologies, if we do not analyze what is right and wrong, good/bad and simply be, then things seem to begin to fit, to gather up their own strength and become clear. And isn't it supposed to be simple, clear — clarity in motion?

If we understand that we are already in the eternal, then there is nowhere to go, no future calamity to be concerned with, no past patterns to be caught in, no greed motivating us, no lust attracting us, no need to get something, to become someone, to be a role we think would be glamorous, no fame attracting us. So then what is the mystic's perspective?

If we are in the natural flow of the moment, right action is not a concept, is not something we need to think about to plan, it is not a way to always act that will always produce the exact result we seek. Instead, we act appropriately to the situation.

If someone is hurt, we help. If we are dirty, we shower. If hungry, we eat. If there is no food to eat, we find food. There is no specific pattern for doing, for this action and non-action. If we are in this state of freedom, where we can go up or down, stand up or sit down, where we can watch the shadows on the wall or play hand puppets, discuss the topics of the day, or be silent, then it becomes a choice of freedom.

Seems if we are in states of bliss, having fun just being, it is our inclination to understand that we are God, all is God, and if another needs our help, we want to help because it is helping ourselves. Serving becomes as natural as breathing because we are serving ourselves, we are adding to the overall good, the radiance of being, we are bringing happiness to all situations with a smile, a gesture, reassurance, understanding, because it is the natural sequence of events to explore our freedom by adding to, becoming one with acting for the sake of acting, and using gentleness to express to others where all should be.

But let's be specific. Say I'm raising an nine-year-old, and say that nine-year-old is becoming agitated, bored, angry, frustrated and so on. Let's say I think I need to disciple him, draw the line. And he takes me to the limits of being patient. And I become stern, angry, strike out to stop his behavior of selfishness, of acting like an nine-year-old. I feel the need to stop the vicious cycle he is caught in. And yet, I feel bad for being the line-in-the-sand he cannot cross. Am I less enlightened because he needs someone to stop his destructive behavior?

There is nothing wrong with being angry, being sad, being the one who says ‘enough is enough.’ Only if I can do it with detached observance. Be the watcher watching the drama instead of believing the serious drama is anything but a guise. And if I can approach, so to speak, all uncomfortable situations with this detached observance, then the bliss comes back, skirts momentarily away, is quickly back again, and we are thus in the flow of perfection, never ever really leaving it.

Appropriate action depends upon appropriate awareness. Be as aware as possible, and the actions are not a “should or shouldn’t,” they just are. They are of the flow, as natural as smiling at a child eating chocolate and ruining their Sunday clothes, as wondrous as understanding that when in absolute states of freedom (meaning when in the present moment fully, not harassed by an illusionary future, not haunted by a disgraceful or challenging past) then we can go this way or that. We can add to the over all good, be the ultimate consciousness that is expressing itself without the delusion of having to place rules and restrictions on what we perceive reality to be, having to act as if we have learned how to act.

A child does not play in a rehearsed way. The dog does not go to the fence and bark in some pattern. The clouds do not float by in some exact jet stream that never changes, and so it is the same with right action. If we are in the flow of the eternal, then we always know appropriate action, and there are no chains to put upon it, no rules to ensnare it.

BE

Chapter 21

Path of Least Resistance

This is when we push and nothing happens, and we pull and nothing happens, but then we just flow around it, whatever It may be, like water flowing around the river rocks.

If we push too hard, become too frustrated, too addicted to a result, then results will avoid us like money does a poor man, like love does the lonely. The more we believe we need something, the less likely we are able to get it. The more we need to get for ourselves, the less we get for ourselves. Yet the more we care not of the result, the more the results will happen like miracles.

Anyone in sales knows the phenomenon too well: When riding the crest of the wave, all is well, people seem to buy and buy some more. But when in a slump, when in our hearts we believe we need to generate income, it flees from us like scared cats on a back fence, like gorgeous women scattering from an ugly-man convention.

We always need to take the path of least resistance. And if there is resistance, it is because we are creating the resistance, we are self-creating the results to flee from us. We are pushing so hard trying to force reality through a tube, make it happen. And surely we can make it happen at the expense of long-term damage, at the expense of others' feelings, another's attitude, and so on.

The path of least resistance is the flow of being, is realizing that if there is no place to get to, we might as well stay right here and let the results happen and come up to us, manifest themselves of their own volition rather than having a scheme, a plan, a way things must fit. We need to give room to all the perplexities — room to breathe, room to have alternatives come to the game of life. We need to not grasp in order to get, not hold to hug, not desire to be flooded and graced with so much, enough of the All (and this includes money).

The path of the least resistance is riding the crest of the wave and not trying to project a desire, not trying to get to point A. Simply, our **being** is getting enough. Be, and point A will come along just fine. Be not fretful about what you believe must happen, and what does happen is fine, perfect, enough, the right direction for the flow to meander through and take us, too. All suffering is in the expecting of something we want to happen, wanting our rigid desires to unfold, and then they don't. Thus, the wanting of This or That to happen and it doesn't, really is where most of our suffering truly lies. If we are able to flow around obstacles instead of taking them as serious roadblocks getting in the way of what we want, then we can maneuver, turn right or left, or smile, or stop and watch the eagle circling overhead, or let the sweetness in the breeze add love and gentleness to all situations no matter if the tension is flying through the air or the Phoenix is rising up from the pyres.

Practice the path of least resistance to accomplish more, to stand or sit or lay in the eternal moment, to understand that the flow will take us where we need to go. For it is our clinging, our expectations of a result, our desire to be somewhere else, to get to that next moment and the next moment and so on that causes the ultimate frustration, the tension, the battles within.

It is not what is happening that is crucial; it is how we react, respond, merge with what is happening that is natural. All else causes us severe pain where we hand over the freedom we are always seeking.

To be free we must drift with the flow, sit in the boat, watch the drama as a drama, believe we are adding to the overall good, that we are actually (ourselves) the overall good, that we are adding momentous bliss back to the huge absolute consciousness that is, and we can merge with it. Then we can share our consciousness with others. And that simplicity of consciousness, that gentleness arising, that placid inner peace is what accomplishes all we ever need, and that this gentleness will soothe the weary on their rocky paths, it will create true friendships, will massage the eternal into the bones of the musclebound and tense lifters of harsh reality.

Our inner peace can create bliss, happiness, can manifest all that we need if we do not force it, do not name it, do not try to manipulate a selfish result, and if we realize, no matter what, no matter how seemingly bad the situation may appear to ourselves or to others, that when taking the path of least resistance, when going with the flow, when letting God, when action and non-action coincide, are one, when we be and enjoy the being no matter what, not because we are told to, not because it is a belief, but when we be and enjoy the being, then all the elusive and wondrous things come sniffing up around our legs. All the scared become fearless. All the tension evaporates into a mist of calm, all this tension or stress is replaced with peace. All the walls come tumbling down and we see options in responding, options in alternative paths to take, options to smile and walk away, or walk around or become infatuated with the actual drama of the This and That, but still keeping a detached distance, and just have a **such-ness** inside and outside that keeps us focused on the present. For when we sit fat in the eternal, nothing can touch us, not the aggravation, not the viciousness of the so-it-seems outer world. And if we slip up and get annoyed, become frustrated, lose our temper or our control of our bliss, it just happens.

Yet, we are getting better and better as we walk in our inner peace, though at times we may slip up, we may forget, we may again respond as we have been incorrectly taught to respond. But if we know in our beings that this is true, that we are peaceful by nature, we will very seldom be thrown off the surfboard as we ride the wave, only occasionally will we be thrown off the horse as we ride and gallop through/in eternity.

The path of least resistance is the natural and absolute flow of eternity burgeoning up and recreating itself until there becomes no "until" in our minds at all. When we can stay in our peacefulness forever and smile as we see through the illusion others are caught inside...as we see others go in and out of the place, this place, that no one can ever — in actuality — leave, then we begin to understand.

Chapter 22

Living in the Present

We have been taught our entire lives to get somewhere, to make something of ourselves, to create a magical future, a place to be, a kind of distancing of ourselves from this present moment, so much so that we have conditioned ourselves that we never have enough, never should be satisfied, that we should "get out of our comfort zones," push on and on to be more and more.

We have, in the USA, this country of materialism, lost the art of being, of living without a future, without a past, of being absolutely satisfied with all that is, all that comes our way, satisfied to work when we work, to sit when we sit, play when we play, to let time shed its illusion. We have so much so conditioned ourselves to believe in a better world...someday, to get to heaven, to find the gold we are always searching for...and thus, we have lost the peacefulness in just existing, in enjoying the complete and fat moment.

For many, if we do not believe in a future, in a result, in a "getting somewhere," then we cannot live in this state of perfection. Thus, we have no motives, no desires, no place to get to, nothing to accomplish. This can become unnerving, because we have for so long conditioned our minds, our beings to chase a bright and rosy future that will, we hope, manifest someday.

The future is now. We have arrived! Utopia is happening right now. Someday came.

Those who can enjoy the moment are those who have the entire universe by the tail, are those who can swim in the eternal moment and not be nudged or manipulated or chained to a "somewhere to get to."

Granted, we have things to do, places to go, events to participate in, we have weddings to attend, meetings to sit through, clocks to watch, sunrises and sunsets to admire, grief to feel, details to take care of...the slipping and sliding of the NOW moment through what appears to be a constant set of circumstances that seem to forever change...but that is the illusion.

This moment is forever, this one, single, complete, never-ending, absolute, eternal moment where God exists. It is just the appearance of change that makes us want to get to another point in time instead of being in this forever point in time...or out of time, depends how you look at it.

The art of true living is in the realizing that this point in time is all we have, all we shall ever have, and to treat it as one eternal pinpoint of change. If we ride it like a wave, continue in it, be It, then all the changes, all the situational comedies and tragedies, all the so-called dramas going by become mere skins of the snake shedding, merely the forever movie moving through one actual point in time that is always the same eternal point in time. And thus, if we learn to be in this point in time, this actuality, then there is absolute peace, truth, beauty, always-ness that protects us from our self-created fantasies that entice us and/or threaten us into apprehensive states of worrying about a nonexistent future or some ridiculous confining past. Don't get all bottled up like that.

We can be eternal beings in this eternal moment, only if we care not for a result, care not for who or what comes in and out of our lives, if we love and be kind to all the fantasies being spun around us.

There really are no problems; it is the mind that thinks hard about a problem, and what emotional abysses we should partake in. These thoughts (usually upsetting) are what try to get us here or there. And when it doesn't happen as we envision, then we become frustrated or depressed because we are trying to get to a self-created, usually (never actualized) at least ephemeral, future. Instead, be in the eternal moment. Be blissful. Because in our hearts, we know we can absolutely be happy right now, not tomorrow, not next week, not after we become a doctor or a lawyer or after we inherit that money we think someone might've left us. Be blissful at this pinpoint of reality — that will always be the key.

Freedom comes from this simple realization, and thus, we can have fun in sheer new experiences rather than to believe in new experiences that may happen some other day.

So many talk, have talked, of cosmic consciousness, the highest states of bliss, of being, of actualizing. If and when and as we become the moment, feel this peace in the certainty of this moment, then we are blissful little doodads, children at play, not worried, not heavy with the proclaimed seriousness of adulthood, not fretting over anything we believe we so desperately need.

This does not mean we should never think, never plan, never use our rational minds to figure out that our job is not flowing along because we need to hire a new secretary, or we need to analyze a situation, to find out if there is something that would flow better, contemplate ways to relax in the tension of modern stressfulness. But, as we understand that the planning is just a game, something to play around with, not the thing itself, not this moment itself, we then find our peace.

True happiness is getting enough sleep, attending to that which makes the human body balanced: good food, exercise, things that help us actualize the present with feel-good stuff. And as we do, have fun in our doing, play to play, be to be, sit to sit, rationalize to rationalize, discuss to discuss, eat to eat, walk to walk, meditate to meditate, then all things are not a string of events, not a linear timeline but, rather, a moment to exist forever, to find our bliss, our passions, dig up new roads on old maps to follow to the edge of a new perception, experience new avenues on the Boulevard, watch the naked girl being painted in the back studio by some mad artist, see the sun gathering light over a new morning horizon, see the comet zooming yet static at 40,000 miles an hour, see the trees pop out of their buds and their dreamy winter's sleep.

Living in the present moment is all that we can do, all we need to do (it is easy to get a degree in — no special training required). And yet, if we try too hard, it becomes false, like thinking about living in the present moment, like wandering around not knowing what to do, like trying to figure out how to dance rather than just dancing, or having someone teach improvisational comedy to a serious mind, or to play improvisational piano by the book, by written music. So then we mistakenly think that by believing there is no future, then, of course, there is nothing to do. And we can get caught in a kind of static moment and can't figure out what to do. Again, we are thus pretending to live in the moment, worried that we might be actually getting it wrong, fretting about not knowing what to do. Does the child ask how to run in the backyard and play with the dogs? Does the toddler starting to walk worry about falling? Does the fox running through the fields of wild flowers forget to listen to the startling sounds of prairie dogs or the Labrador barking down the valley?

Pure awareness does not need a reason, a motive, does not need to find itself. It is itself. It is action in its purest sense. It is truth in being. It is following an inclination, a bit of intuition, sleeping when tired, working when work should be done. It has no prejudiced attitudes toward what is fun versus what is mundane, what is good to do, what is simply recreational therapy, what is a struggle or what is enjoyed, or what is just cleaning toilets.

All action is a movement, a strain of muscle, a retraining of the mind to be, to focus on the events, attending to the life force that is, should be, can be celebrated in each and every situation, whether shopping for groceries or being personally acknowledged as the greatest gift in a respected profession by colleagues on a sunny afternoon in some park in the delightful spring foothills.

The circumstance does not matter; it is not the concern here, not what must be done compared to what we want to do; it is not that we are chained to present bill paying or that we can take a cruise to the Bahamas tomorrow. Each moment, each event should be seen as a cruise, as a thank-God-I-am-still-above-ground, a wondrous experience.

Though we should think and act out the things we love to do, we should, also, act and do the things we feel we must do with the same expectation of bliss, of an underlying perfection taking hold.

With this attitude, all problems dissolve.

And what is a problem? What really is a problem, anyway? Is it not a situation (any event) we somehow feel we do not like and must get away from? Like going to the dentist, or a business we feel we must struggle at to make more money at, or a bill that can't be paid but must (in our minds), or a friend who is sick, or we are sick, or a car breaks down, or we have an argument with someone about something absurd.

So what are the problems we have had to deal with? Are they not simply letting our calm mind fret, get upset, an emotional upheaval when we could've remained calm, placid? And we could have simply done what we should've done to resolve something that somehow appears, on the surface, a problem. And a problem, is it not but our reaction at this present moment to something we fear in a future that will not come? This is what is causing all the turmoil inside.

The only problem, or should we say exciting challenge, we will ever have is how to remain focused and aware of this divine moment that is always with us, how to feel the immense energy of this perfect moment that is our absolute security, to know this one perfect moment is not some present experience going by like a marching band, like events and people and problems.

Instead, we need to realize this one, absolute, perfect moment is God himself, is All, and that the All is here for us, protecting us, shielding us from the pain, from the illusion that is rolling by.

Partake in God or illusion, that is the simple choice we need to make each and every single moment (of what we refer to as our existence). Then God will protect us, be with us, not in some church, not in some secluded moment as we pray in our rooms, but God will be with us right now. **The "right-now" part of life is God, is the divine,** is the eternal,is all we really have ever needed. The rest is illusion pretending to be important or something we must and are and have to be involved in. This is the falseness of life.

Be God, and God will be us, then we are feeling the complete oneness of the universe. This is as simple as it gets.

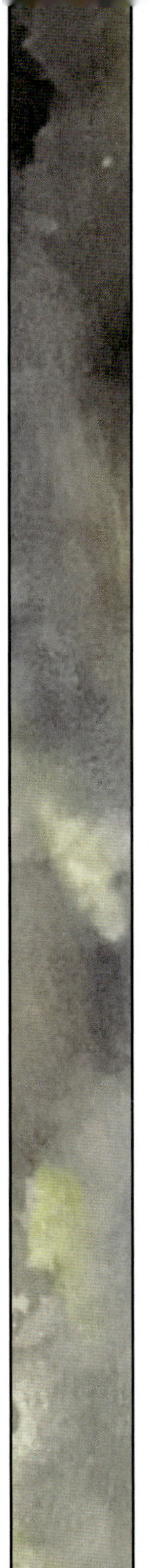

BE

BE

Chapter 23

Who Do We Believe?

Is there a boss, an attorney we admire, a minister who can steer us the right way, a grandmother, a father who might be able to tell us which way to turn? Even these words carry a tainted point of view, strangled words that may or may not get through.

The wondrous thing about life is that we all have a chance, the same chance, can all be our own teachers, can find bliss inside, outside, can get to it as the sages did, as Jesus did, as the holy ones have before us. We need no guidance, no one to be an authority for us, no one to direct our enlightenment. We are all enlightened, we just may not know it, have not actualized it, have not believed little old me could be enlightened, always happy. It can only be for the sages, for those with the intelligence to comprehend such a thing.

This is where the falseness comes in. There is no outer authority, no one to tell us the tales, or explain which paths to follow that will get us there. We are already there, are already sages in robes, already good guys with white hats, already on our way, in the hay, filled with the spirit, on the crest of the wave. We are already there, and there is here and here is supreme bliss, drinking shots of tequila with old friends, slamming down beers, or simply sitting by the spring window and watching the last snow come falling down.

We must be ever so careful who we obtain our advice from, who we let be a giant influence in the small parts of our lives. We must question any authority because, after all, they are us and we are them and who are they to slice up life for us and serve us up what is true, what is right and wrong, tell us who to befriend, who to avoid, which way to turn, which way to run?

Of course, there seems to be an evolving-ness, stages to go through, maturation, developing our own sense of being, an inner goodness or confidence, a way of walking lightly through the chaos, and getting to our own conclusions. And it is as if we are born without this tether of the ego, a baby hardly, if at all, realizing it is a separate being. Then this fledgling is taught to be, or somehow becomes, a separate consciousness. Then our entire lives we strive to become, again, like the baby: Part of everything. And when we finally begin to grasp this, then we expire, become the oneness we have so long avoided in youth, in our driven years.

Though so many have gone before us, we can read and learn and see how they are all saying the same thing: Eradicate the line of subject versus object. The wall needs to come down. We need to realize our eternalness. We are spirits in the material, and so on.

It is good to read the wise guys, to see that what they are saying is what we already know, is exactly what they have been trying to tell us, is what we found out on some starry night as some comet in the sky ran rapture through us like a scimitar in the hand of a marauder. And thus, we became all the answers, all the questions melted into an obvious all-awareness. We became that which we are, have been a part of for so long.

But beware of those who talk too loudly, talk too much, have the right answers and you better believe them or else you'll burn in hell, else you will not be saved, or else you shall fall short of what is expected.

Heed only words that ring true and even then, heed these words with a grain of salt, with doubt, a healthy skepticism about this person behind closed doors; just beware of reprobates reading comic books and shooting up basement drugs while chanting black magic.

There is no authority except our own voice from within, our own bliss, our own happiness. This inner rapture shall guide us, our feelings of good, our emotional reactions of bliss, of feeling complete. No person, no admired man or woman, can give us that which we must discover on our own.

Diogenes the Cynic was approached one day by the all-powerful Alexander the Great who humbled himself to the wise sage, and asked the ascetic cynic: "I am the most powerful man on earth. I rule countless empires. I have wealth untold. What, oh famed Diogenes, can I do for you?"

And Diogenes, resting in the sun, looked up at the great warrior standing over him and said: "Well, yes, could you move a little to the side as you are blocking the warmth of the sun."

Was this cynical, or was this as real as it gets? We have all that we need. No one can give us anything that we need, and no one, not even the greatest of the sages, or the most powerful, or those held high upon the scale of the incredible can give us what we seek. Only by ourselves can we become focused, happy, blissful. And we should not always admire those with money, power, fame, those who can speak gregariously or eloquently. We are our own authority. And remember, no Alexander the Great can give us that which we already have. This seems to ring true.

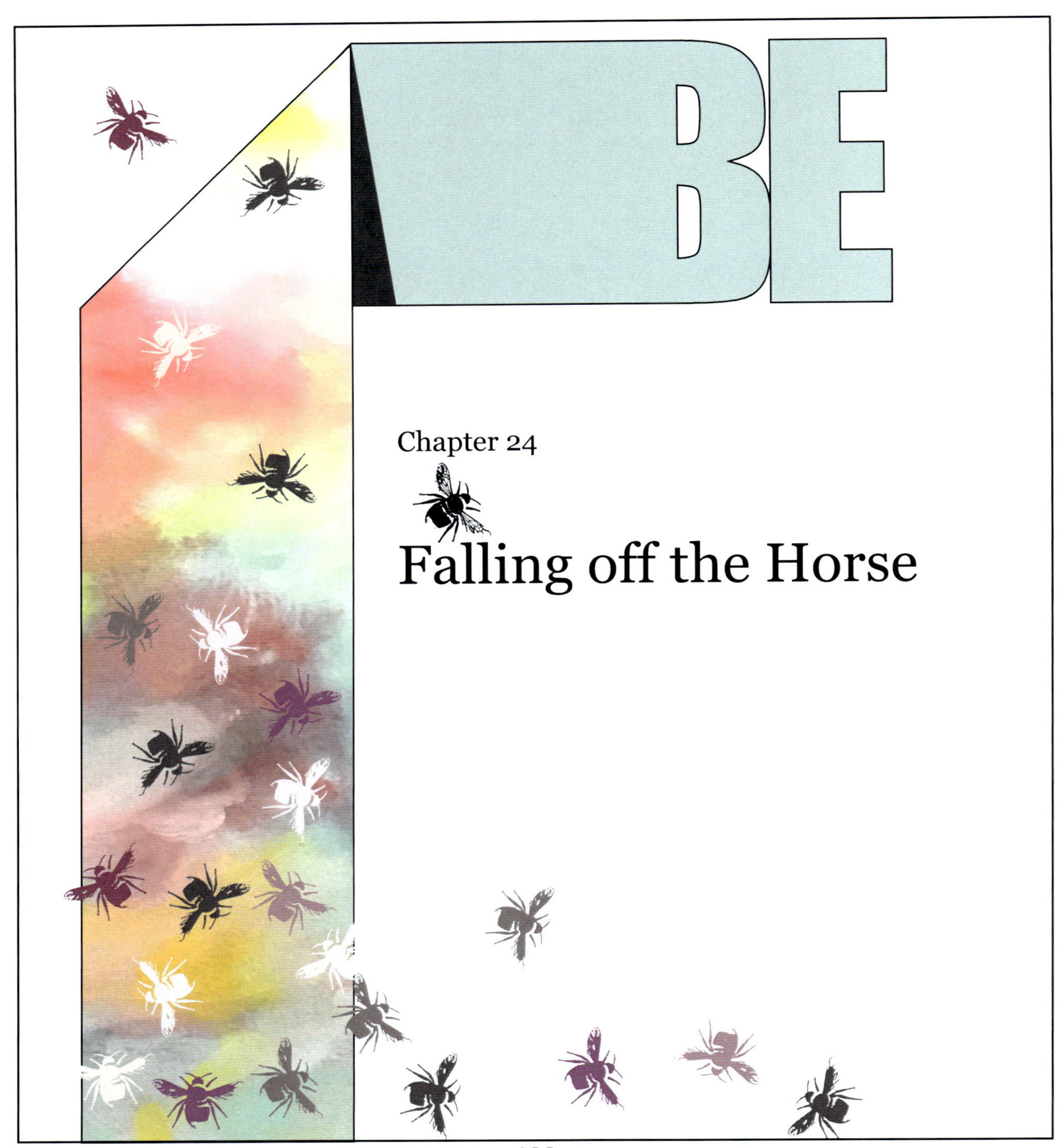

Chapter 24

Falling off the Horse

We all want to and can live in the deeper (higher, more aware) levels of consciousness. But many of us still have emotional addictions, and get lost in an occasional, maybe even a long-winded, tirade where we don't feel enlightened, do not feel like we belong to the cosmic consciousness. What to do?

What else can we do? Work through them, realize we are aborting reality, coming out of the sky to pan for fool's gold. We get lost in a residual of old programming. We are men and women on some journey that took a detour into no-man's land. It's okay. Get a good night's sleep, meditate, try to understand the patterns we throw ourselves in and out of.

The question should not be how we again find ourselves in some emotional mire, but how to climb out of it with dignity; or should we say, how to crawl out of it with a smile and clean underwear.

No matter how far away we get from our bliss, if we slip into a depression, run the gamut of all the negating emotions, get lost on the telegraph wires of some distant past experience (become absurd in the twilight of some bright and sunny day), then it is always the same, always easy, so simple. Mediate, understand, be gentle, realize we do not react perfectly, at least we do not always, at every point, realize our own perfection. Thus, we must find our passage through this brief darkness, be it grief, frustration, anxiety, whatever separating emotions these are, and then finally, simply **get it**. Understand that if we keep awareness heightened, watch what is actually happening, try not to run away, or get into distractions, then we can comprehend it. So find solace in knowing that we are getting better and better, more focused, sage-like, reassured with new and longer levels of bliss.

We may fall off the horse many times before we ride forever into the sunset, until we see the emotional dramas that we are caught in as illusion, and can, at last, let them go faster than cacti grabbed onto by a thirsty man, faster than dust storms forming in Wyoming.

When we fall off our horse, become agitated, out there, it is then we need to see the lessons, find the reasons why we are temporarily, emotionally and psychologically ill. It will pass, but we caused it. We need to own our feelings, find ways to steady the rocking boat, find ways to dissolve these captivating emotions that can actually destroy, debilitate, keep us in patterns of uncomfortable reactions.

And sooner than we think, we begin to see; the fall is short, the ride is long, the world is in a sea of absolute perfection, and so we can be in this state of wondrous bliss most of the time.

All separating emotions can be analyzed, realized that there is a better way. Feel them, then let them go. Don't let these uneasy emotions stick, stick us to wall, to a reason to be sick and tired of some emotional roller coaster we have somehow started and can't get off.

All that we need is right here. There is no place to get to. It is easy once we realize that there is no emotion that we cannot overcome (instead of succumbing to it). There is no bliss that cannot last, or at least that we cannot get back to...and ride into the shimmering silver dawn.

There really are only two states of being: bliss, and all that other stuff we dredge up from our emotional abyss.

If we are focused, in the flow, ageless, timeless, of the perfection, then all is well. Yet, if we are greedy little doodads, wanting something, worried about something, craving recognition, needing more, wanting more, feeling we must be right, needing to have more money, or to fight off the demons feeling hate, anger, seeming to need to get involved in that which doesn't require us to be involved, then we seem to be, feel separated, miserable, elongated and bad. We become a potful of bad emotions that keeps us away from our true natures.

Be at peace, or be at war. There very well may be no in-betweens, just continual bliss, radiance, rapture, smiles, play, or this quiet desperation or being lost in some gut-wrenching emotional drama that we have learned so well to dwell in.

It really is a choice. But we should not feel bad or guilty or recoiled when we fall off the horse, just realize we, for a while, will fall off the horse. So we need to get back up there and begin riding, always being, always riding.

And what do we really want in the everlasting flow of this eternal moment? Do we want hate, fear, emotional deviances, irritability? Or would we rather have love, freedom, creativity, humor, tension-free slipping away into the soft part of a good night?

We can make an instant choice to be, or not to be, to fight the reactiveness of our emotional outbursts or see, in this exact instant, the perfection of all things. It really doesn't have to be some uphill, strenuous struggle. It can be as simple as an insight, a reassurance that we are all things, that the world is user-friendly, that we are already in possession of the gold and it cannot be taken away except by our own greed, our own fighting inside to get something that is false. Instead, we can be blissful, ride the galloping, trotting or still horse. Stay up there. We can be in the deeper levels of consciousness if we simply believe we can, thus do the good and the fun things like smile, meditate, watch the world go gently by, sleep well, eat well and feel the incredible universal energy in this pinpoint moment of so-called time, instead of worrying about all the things that almost never happen. Such a horrendous and difficult choice to make, is it not?

Footnote: The horse, us, the world, the cloudy day, the shy beautiful young girl sitting on some red afternoon porch in a sundress...it is all us. Everything that comes and goes, in and out, is us. There really is no horse to stay up on, just an analogy, and if stretched too far, made to fit too snuggly, all analogies break down, break away from the real bread of reality.

So to stay up on the horse is to be, and be, and be some more. It is all about going back to all the precepts that we have discussed and wind them up into a ball and stall for more time, remind ourselves that we are here, it is here, all that is magical, fanciful, fantastic, all that is phosphorescent, demanding, unyielding, unsurpassed, all that is in the center, stark and naked and sensual, all that slips away and comes in through the back door, is and seems not. All that can be, was, should be, might be, will be. Every possibility, found or lost, is a creation of this NOW moment. There really is nothing else.

The rest is a game we play, an enactment of something that appears sacred, divine, too far out to see without drugs, too near to see without a microscope, too obvious to miss. It is all a perplexity, dueling paradoxes, time and sound and space and things vying for a place upon the shelf in this world.

The point is that we can and must and will ride the horse, because the horse is us. We cannot fall off our own selves. And if we do, it is a game we are mentally playing, a tortuous experiment gone awry, spider legs on the good doctor.

Sure, this last part is written to tear down the walls of logic, of perception, to help struggle with the poetic weave, the last and longing part of something that only exists in the minds of the temptresses and high priestess and vileness inside the coat of someone walking along the surreal plains of vision and conquest.

What I mean is not what can be noted in the cliff notes of some long manuscript before the days of knights and tender maidens in distress, unclean, with dirty teeth and cloth-sort-of sanitary napkins. It is not that absurdity is dirty water in a clear moment. It is more that limiting words that try and explain truth is like fishing without a hook, catching dreams in a sieve, draining out the life force for a slow-cooked goat on Easter as the Italian traditions make us eat meat.

Falling off the horse is the biggest of all illusions. It is only felt when we have fallen, but we cannot fall because we are the horse. So in order to get back up and ride, we must precisely realize there is no horse and then get back up ride the hell out of life, a knife between the teeth, a foreskin and foreplay move on some chest board of a pair of virgins on parade.

Now that we have this cleared up, let's move on?

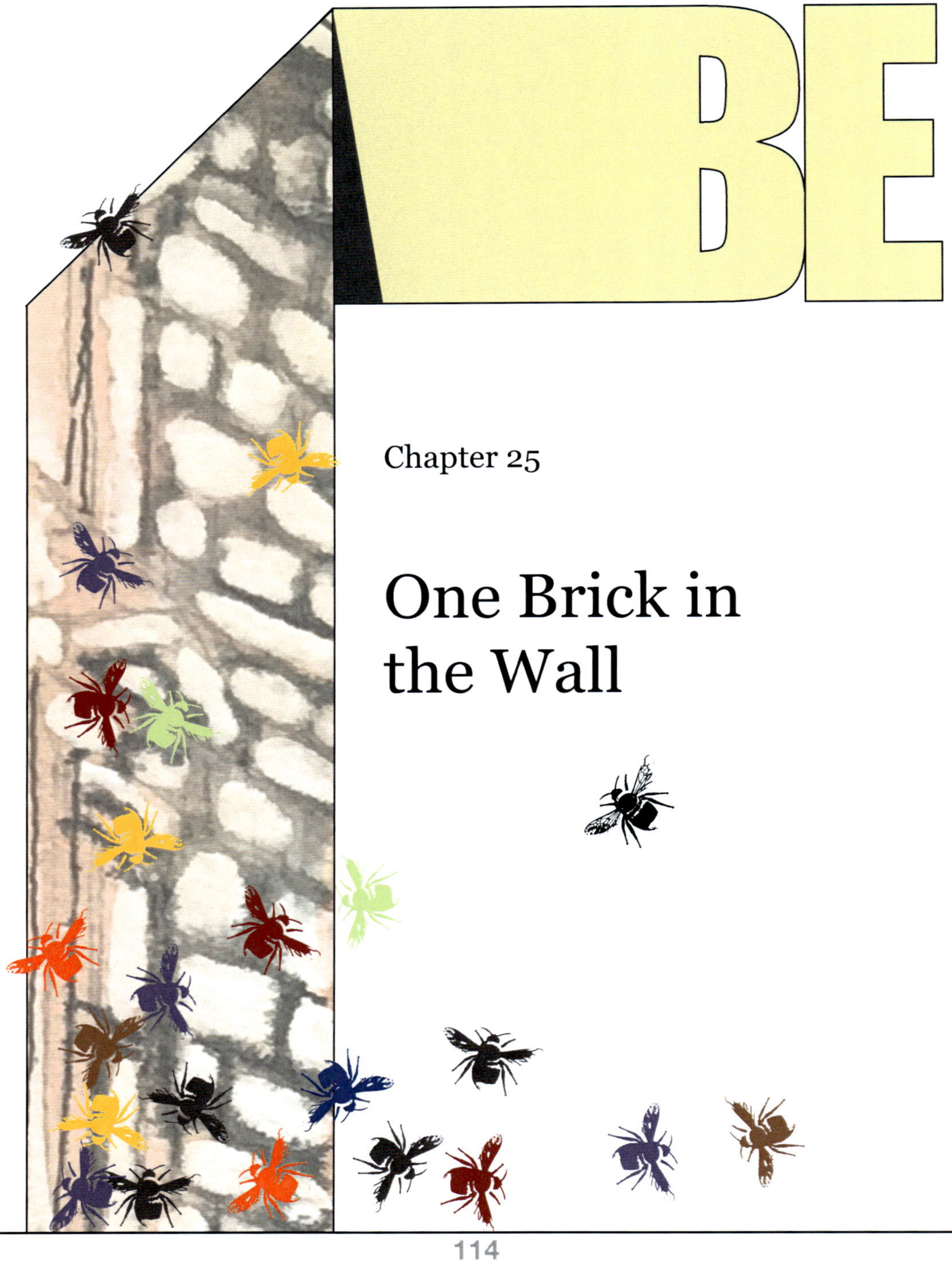

BE

Chapter 25

One Brick in the Wall

Of all the suffering, all our emotional battering, trying to get what we want, or getting out of the way of what we don't want, finding peace, creating no peace, going here and there, putting up more fences to cage in the wrong, keep in the right, all that puts "right" in front of "wrong," opposites inside and against some kind of conflict...all things that can tear down, convolute, confuse, refuse, all that can denigrate, disintegrate, is all able to be simply destroyed in one stroke of the Zen, one quick little realization: We are here, and this is all we need.

The eternal moment is perfection in motion. We need no other "getting to it." Nothing can hold us down, harm us, but our own illusion to be happy, to get somewhere, to recreate a horrific past, or create a tempting future. It is the illusion we propagate that snags inside something that we want to get out of: There is nothing to get out of. Nowhere to get to. No perfection to find. It is right here, right now, always, and all we are doing, have been doing, is trying to separate ourselves from this forever Caesarean birth of pain and pleasure.

Most do not want to be born again, not quite yet, maybe later in the wee hours of some kerosene-inspired late night, maybe after college, after a slug of good wine, maybe pretty soon. We cling so hard to our illusions like they were sustenance, food to eat by, light to see by, wine to drink.

We really are able to pull out the one brick that blocks us from all the perfection. Do it now, this instant, and all the rest, all the rest of the illusion will fall away like skin peeling off a dead man, like a generous portion of mashed potatoes served up on some Mississippi plantation, like word games played by all the wordsmiths shooing away the tenderness of love and this moment that will never end.

The biggest problem we all have is that we say to ourselves we will do it later, be complete and blissful and happy later, find the right moment in a while, 'cause we still have so much to do, so many obligations to fill like prescribed drugs. We have so much we should do instead of doing what we love to do, too many fears to overcome, too many neuroses to put in a grab bag and pull out later.

With one quick pull of the lowest brick in the wall, we can make it all tumble down and breathe the fantastic air, see the sunshine stream through the bars on the window that aren't holding us in there anymore. So easily can we stop the emotional pain that seems ever so real.

This is no joke, no little concept to keep us warm at night, no blithering in the blizzard of some hazy bunk.

We can see – if we simply be, learn how to be — that all that we have ever strived for, ever needed is coagulating in front of our very eyes. The universe of billions of galaxies is at this instant, with us.

We are at the outer edge of the farthest galaxy, yet, we are here, we are it and it is us: The motion in the trees, the flocks of birds gathering in the sky, the wonder why, the truth, the All-ness is here with us, not in the bathroom, or in a minute, or soon to be on TV, but it is with us NOW, in this flash, this very moment we are doing anything. We are the doing, can become the doing. It is the doing.

Call it God, call it truth, beauty, wondrousness, goodness; no matter what the name, what label we feel inclined to affix to it...It is! And we can swim in it as if it were a whirlpool of "just-right" tepid water, wear it as if it were an old pair of jeans or hot underwear pulled out of the dryer on a cold morning. It was, is, will always be...right here.

This actuality, this simplicity, can tear down every wall we have ever psychologically built between us and them, between fate and destiny, between happiness and dullness, between anything that separates us at this moment, from God, from, as I love to say, the burgeoning, all-gushing-forth of the volcano of this complete, satiated moment that we can guide, like a golden ship, to wherever we want it to take us.

Happiness is not complacency, not lethargy on the couch of some afternoon dysfunctional TV, not a strenuous getting to, finally believing after years of study and work that we may get a tiny glimpse into the ultimate reality of all things. No! It is right now, right here, in all people's grasp.

Simply thinking about it is like revving up the engine, like, at least, coming over to touch the face of the beautiful princess as she sleeps, inching toward that which is laughing behind our backs, saying, "Hey, they'll see us if they simply open their eyes. They'll find us if they quit searching so hard. Hey, they'll become us if they quit trying to become something else they've been taught to try to become by someone else," like a good doctor, a waitress, a businessman, a high-grade student, a clean wife, a dedicated husband — anyone trying so hard to fit into that which we can fit into easily if we didn't believe we had to be as someone else told us to be.

So the way, the actual simplest way, the only way to remove the bottom brick from all our suffering, to make the walls fall down and away, to make "the bottom of the bucket fall out," the sky to fall on us like rose petals in a flower parade, is to be. Simply be and let our being take us into more tranquil states of being: going to go, eating to eat, drinking to get drunk and to have some fun, getting angry to get angry, and (this is most important) to watch a part of us that is not getting involved. Stay close to the part of us that is not getting involved, the eternal part that just witnesses, just smiles at the drama, does not attempt to stop the drama, does not attempt to run from the drama, but attempts to watch the drama as if being in the audience instead of being the sweating, star actor on stage with the hot lights upon him, going through the pain and the strife.

Instead, be the audience of your own experience and then the experience becomes a gag, a joke, a good smoke, a motion of the eternal changing shapes, the chameleon parts of the eternal, shadows of sun and moonlight, bits and pieces in the whole production of billions of universes happening right now for our immediate entertainment, a kind of Seward's folly.

Chapter 26

Moving Through the Dream

We are in the perfection of this moment, and we can create from this potential that which we want to come about, that which we want to flourish.

Reality is and always has been. There is an absoluteness to it, something static, the same, reassuring, past the illusions, beyond, perhaps way beyond, speculation. But in the realm of games, of having something to do, can we conjure up energy to form patterns that will manifest? For what purpose is usually a good question. But if we try to benefit all, and we are part of the All, then the All should accommodate us. We can orchestrate the universe to accommodate our dreams if we are approaching all our creating without selfishness, with a perspective to add something good to the patterns of energy we see twisting and turning in some kind of greediness.

The catch-22 is that if there is no place to get to, no reality in the getting somewhere, in creating a future, then why do it at all? That is the big question. But we are a captive audience in the play of life and if we are breathing, living in the patterns of energy, then we should act as if we needed something to do, create experiences that are dumbfounding, that are exciting, see through the illusion but exist to exist, play to play, plan to plan, organize to organize, do to do.

Though results are secondary, though we can ride the crest of the wave and watch ourselves acting out, seem involved, become passionate about our dreams, we do not have to take them too seriously; more like reality is enough, being is enough, the morning is enough, the coolness of this shy dawn is stupendous enough to enjoy as the brightness comes up over the mountains.

The push of the soul is to add some kind of service to the overall human condition, to act like the American Indians and Natives used to, act as if we would be effecting seven generations into the future, find ways to add to the overall good and see through the overall illusion that can do nothing but wreak havoc, create an imbalance in the interaction of things.

Someone once said, "All I can do is support your consciousness." And can that be so far off, so off the mark? We can add energy, good energy, balance, love, kindness, gentleness to the consciousness going on, otherwise we are polluting more than a physical environment.

So all work, all that we seem to elusively pursue, should be directed at pushing onward, toward a support of others on their way home, in their emollient dreams, adding something to get all to work together to create more harmony and see how people are of one race, one planet, one species, one universal energy.

We need to support each other, bind to each other, simply love each other and quit this competitiveness. Not that we shouldn't strive to become better and better, to unwind that which is too tightly wound up inside, but be as focused and balanced as we can; judge not the dream happening. Be not afraid to see the greed, the unrest, the selfish endeavors of those striving so hard to become what is so much illusion, and yet help guide them, maybe through example, maybe through direct confrontation to realize that there is a better way. Gently explain that we can give more than we receive, we can work together, become part of the family of humanity rather than striving for our little purposes and leaving a trail of garbage and misery and pollution and negation wherever we go.

And for those who will not listen, are too thick, who must keep their bleeding noses to the grindstones and get more and get more and get more...well, should we not leave them alone to keep beating their heads against the wall of absurdity, the brick wall of getting some kind of satiation through greed, through selfish and individual pursuit?

It is much like the story of the small child who was asked why he kept beating his head against the wall, and he said, "Because it feels so good when I stop."

Some day the driven, the greedy, will also stop, will see the bad energy they are involved in. And if we cannot dispel their illusion, then they must do it themselves; and maybe again, we should reserve judgment and just do what we envision our highest potential is to do.

We are energy packets who can make a difference in the illusion, who can penetrate the curtain of uncertainty, who can be and add love to the sour soup. We can become and grow and see and change and be blissful little happy guys with bits of dark sides that haunt us occasionally. But we can rebound and be mostly good, mostly enlightened, and yet not be afraid of the sides of ourselves that may be ugly, may be deemed unacceptable.

We are whole, and yet parts of our whole are sometimes ugly, non-acceptable, like feeling angry, being too sexual, wanting to get more, have more, to think that just this once we can be mean and it will finally have a good impact or effect. We too have illusions to play out. But there is a static eternalness that smiles as we become too serious about something that is, after all, a mere illusion...a handful of beans that will dispel the ghosts after a while.

So many think, realize, believe this is a dream, a passing of one state of energy into another. Some entertain the valid thoughts that the universe is incredibly huge, maybe infinite, and we are little white mice trying so hard to run around in our cages. And still the eternal is always with us, sitting with us. Call it God, call it the completeness of each and every moment. So why the rush? Why the frantic pursuit of something that can never be found except by stopping the chase, the pursuit of something that is smiling in the eaves, something that is the dream.

And the static part, the God part, is found so easily by stopping the internal chatter, the inner dialogue. Yet these incessant thoughts are also simply okay to watch as they pass by like a passenger train — just don't let any bad guys, any deep-seated, vicious emotions get off and take you with them.

Watch the flow, the situation. Be the situation. Stay partially uninvolved. Believe in instant enlightenment. Go over there and be erratic, yet stable. See the churning uncertainty but believe in an Absolute. Talk in paradox and parable and realize it may be the only way to define that which is

invisible to the cluttered eye, not there...yet. It is like looking up into the night sky and looking out to the side of something, with the rods of our peripheral vision to see it clearly. But as soon as we, in the dark, try to stare directly at it, it disappears, vanishes, eludes the keenest of eyes, the sharpest of logic.

And it is a vital point to make that we are chasing our own fears, running so fast away from that which we think will grab us, get us: the bogeyman, the intangibles streaming in from some illogical neurosis.

There is nothing chasing us, no monsters under the bed, no tragedies up ahead, nothing that we cannot handle, cannot rise above. So be not fretful of all the phantoms in the night, the demons in our own brains. For we are fish swimming in the eternal ocean and can go here or there, can breathe underwater, can survive the earthquake, the tornadoes, the twisters, the ugly parts of some illusion merely passing by.

Our greatest quality is our humanity: to love, and give and believe that things are getting better, to understand that it is this pinpoint of the present where all the needs are fulfilled, where the demons cannot find us, where the imagination can flow, the wine can flow, the inspiration can flow, the future can become ignited with hope, where the past cannot bind us, where the enjoyment of friends, sex, beauty, of all the truth we can handle is so very ever-present and everlasting.

So as the dream goes by, it is our logic that stops us, our uncontrolled, un-owned thoughts that bind us. It is our persistence and attractiveness to get deeply involved without a buffer zone, our belief that that which is happening in front of our eyes is the only truth and we must lament or become concerned with it to the point of no control. And yet, even if we seem to fall apart, fall away from the God-ness happening, we can still remain in place, in a focused place, an always-lit candle in the wind, a blowtorch in any hurricane.

BE

Chapter 27

The Art of Being

And what is so important? What is it we are so apprehensive about? What is our mission, our destiny, our reserved notion about perplexing things that govern our attitudes, thoughts, actions, the state of inertia that keeps us going in one direction, day after day, afraid to go in any other direction?

We are free to float, to eat goat, to drift or to drive, to become or be, to hang on, hang loose, or hang it all out...but the key, the door that will begin to open, is the perception of one's own comprehending, the sense of being after all the dust clears, all the words lose meaning, all the leftovers are thrown out.

Bottomline: Why not be experts at being, at enjoying the flux? Get involved with (but always reserve your right to laugh at) the absurdity. See the peripheral things happening that are us, are unnoticed by the intense ones on a mission to accomplish their agendas.

To be, to sit fat in our own sense of being, this is all that is really important. All other things run up to us like lost wanderers in the spectrum of what seems to be going on. And all things will be attracted to us if we will only be, add lightness to the overall serious throes of life, if we will simply add a good joke to some techno babble, if we will befriend those who are cast out, if we will add some certain kindness to the grab bag games we seem to love to play and invent.

Our goal in life shouldn't be to get a pile of money or things, or to live in the mansion on the hill, should not be to gather our influence and popularity on the surface of some shallow play, should not be to build castles in the air, but to be. Be so comfortable with who we are that we attract others to see us as shining light, gems in the rough becoming polished. Then others can see us as real, unencumbered, absolute, able to flow and go and walk naked amidst the fresh falling snow.

We need to be the example of being, play with reality as it has so seemingly played with us, as we have let it play with us, let life call the shots, others lay down the laws. And yet, we have always been in charge, in this absolute freedom, able to drift or float or serve or give and love and act appropriately because we are in the mother's womb, cannot fallout, like a marsupial in a flesh pocket, a baby kangaroo being carried to some oasis of a star-studded night as the wind sifts through the palm trees.

Sometimes poetry is all that can help us get there. All words can do is put up a few signposts, reminds us of the memory of it, help us get far away from words and near the bone, the meat, the passionate tingling of reality happening in all places all at once, at all times, in all space, a volcano of eternal eruptive change. And we are not only watching it go by, but we become **the going by** ourselves. We need to go nowhere because we are everywhere without leaving home. We are free to go or stay, to enjoy or to get lost in the emotions or the ripples of thoughts that can take us over there, where there is there, where there is no “over there” at all, just a moment in time and space that can be transcended by being, and by nothing else.

The art of being is at the core of all mystic pursuit, the destination where the train stops. A place where the clamoring of fools talk in riddles about things that are but masks or curtains and paradox. And yet, the simplicity of it is so pervasive that all things are connected to this absolute being-ness.

As the sages, all the happiest of idiots, all the greatest of comics, all the ones of seemingly intense direction and incredible fruitfulness are all guided by this one and simple artifact of humanity that is handed down and handed down: the art of being.

There are so many ways to practice this **being** stuff: Walk and see. Feel the legs, the motion of existence in the breathing. See the patterns of ice crystals on the bay window. Watch the geese fly over and scatter and honk in the cloudy sky. Sense the intense life-force thriving in each cell of the body. Listen intently, trying to understand another’s reality wholly. Smile at the trees budding. Sit quietly near a river and see the spray of water coming off the rocks. Envision all things as yourself as they’re streaming by like the chimes in the church, the train whistle blowing and echoing in the heart of the dark night, the roll of car tires, yes, all is me, completely me.

All happenings are part of this being, of realizing the connective-ness, the tissue and the cartilage that holds all things together, keeps us in this pool of wondrous, pleasant, obvious, enlightened, perfect...eternity.

M. Dowling 6/18

Chapter 28

Fun?

So I am talking to Mark who runs a bike shop, and I ask him, "How are you? Are you having fun?" And he smiles and says, "Sure, what else is there?"

Shouldn't that be our mission...daily, to have fun? Add to each moment a spoonful of peace to the cosmic consciousness, act enlightened, believe there is no becoming, no time, no space, nowhere to go? But still remind ourselves to play the overall conceived-of games as if they were important, as if it meant something, as if there was no other game in town.

Part is focusing on one thing to create a reality. The biggest part is merely having fun, realizing this is the moment of the everlasting moment and God is with us and all we need to do is do, and all we need to accomplish is what we need to accomplish, and all that we need to worry about is nothing, and all that we need to interpret are the dead sea scrolls, and all we need to map out is breakfast, or brushing our teeth, maybe map out a fun plan for the day that might or might not end in profit, may or may not unravel into the most illustrious dream ever conceived of by a human to date.

One of the greatest sages of the 20th century, Krishnamurti, loved to read mysteries or detective novels or something like that, meaning all the high philosophy is nothing but baggage on the last train out.

It is all about having fun. The sunshine is not serious. The birds do not complain. The river doesn't think which way to flow. The grass doesn't question when to start to become green in the spring. And are humans not the same — part of a part, cyclical in nature, happy by decree, intense in intense moments, emotional at limited times, and peaceful sitting all alone in some quiet spot?

We need to be blissful, extract any worry, get rid of any residual fear that hinders us from dreaming the greatest of dreams, from attempting to scale the highest mountains, or simply sitting in the basement and staring at spiders on the wall.

Peacefulness, true and absolute and deep peacefulness, is not misery on the phone home, is not cancer and sterile hospital beds, is not, "Someday I'll be where I want to be." No, peacefulness is right now, is intense blissfulness as we stroll along the slippery edges of a new perception, or the sharp and jagged edge of something dangerous yet full of opportunity calling.

Fun is usually associated with an occasion, an event, a party, a play, a place to go, to go experience it. When in reality, fun is a rolled up packet in the pocket of the everyday man. Fun is morning breath with a twist of lime, is a cup of coffee near a window as the spring snow rains down. Fun is now, in the car listening to music, is skipping stones on the lake of perfection, is all that is, visiting us and staying over for the night, is here today and gone never, is in the rearview mirror, is in front of us, is to the side of us. Fun is what we should aim for and then put the gun down and just pet it, feel it quivering in our bones, see it everywhere. Fun can be seen climbing the tree, inventing new rhymes, editing our lives to only keep the best parts which pretend to have been, pretend to someday be, but are with us right now.

Enlightenment is not a concept. It is...and is and is and is. What else is there, anyway?

We need to feel the disconcerting emotions and hurry up and get back to fun (or blissfulness might be the best word to use here).

So often, when things seem to be going awry, when the mind is full of wonder why's, confusion is thicker than a bear rug, we thus abstract into some Utopian world we think is ideal for us: maybe being in a secluded cabin in the mountains, growing vegetables, reading poetry and weaving, or buying some glittering, central-Californian, ocean home and watching the whales migrate to Mexico. And yet, simply being in the universal Utopia of our own minds is all that we crave. Utopia is NOW, it is just cluttered with social convention, bad laws, street signs, dystopia, misunderstood neurosis on the path of more neurosis and screwed up priorities. But in actuality, the Utopian world is here with us. God is with us. Enlightenment is with us. Being is with us. All that we need is with us. And, then, after we realize this simplicity, we can work from this premise to act as if we are creating a future, buying land in the Ozarks, calling up the powers that be, because you've perfected the art of being.

Peacefulness should not be our goal, it should just be realized, understood. It is not something that can be attained, it simply is. And if we want to realize our part of the Is, then all we need to do is grab hold, let go, become, see it, feel it, don't chase it, but capture it, ride it, notice it everywhere in everything and then, the fun will begin not at some future party, not on some envisioned wedding day, not soon to be, but the fun will begin right now. And then we can smile at all the games we've been taught to play and see through them, and, instead, watch the summer breeze fluttering through the chiffon curtains as the moonlit night is actually a state of becoming and an act of being at the same time. And then we can see It in the sounds, hear It in the snow falling, add paradox to nonsense and come up with a solution that mixes well in a martini, that divulges its secret like magicians on the sunset veranda, like alchemists in purple robes smiling at frog legs, eyeing the newt, like all things religious, divine, arcane and undercover, creating this coming together to form a union where separation is an illusion, where truth is right now and beauty is found under any rock we choose to look under.

Have fun, be happy, be complete, be, and the rest of the world has no choice but to accommodate us, has no choice but to fall in line, has no other choice but to shyly admit to all of us that they, the world, the 10,000 Things, the seemingly separate things, were always one, big, good friend with the keys to the city, with the answers which we have always seemed to seek somewhere else; it is exactly like befriending a gnome for an Irish treasure map, or slipping a twenty to a leprechaun that has magical powers and can guide us to fabled cave of gold.

This absolute good, this perfection, this Utopia we all seek is in this exact second. Go no farther and all will open up like a table set for hundreds, like an oasis appearing in the driest part of some formidable desert, like everything we have always wanted and envisioned...but so much more.

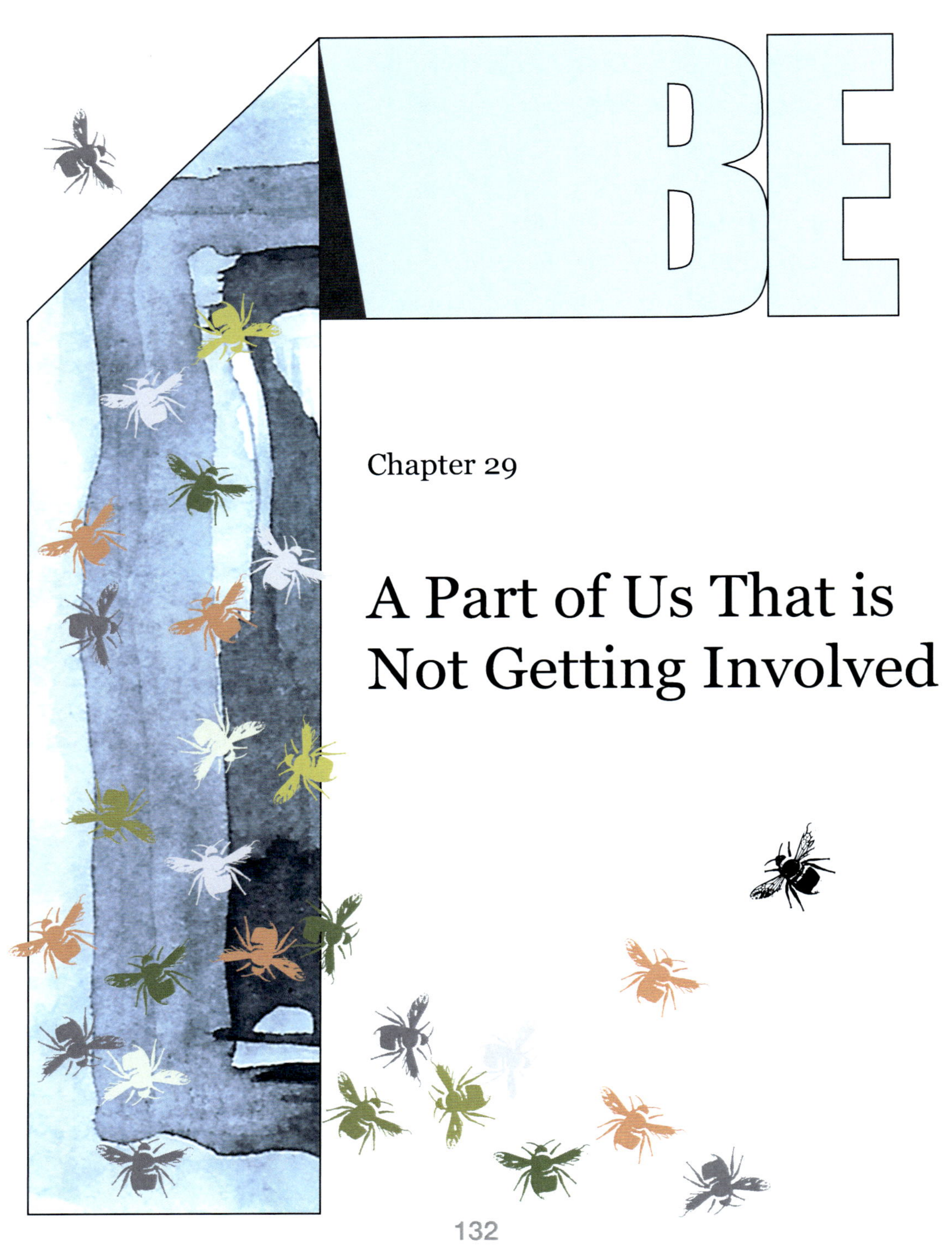

Chapter 29

A Part of Us That is Not Getting Involved

Ken Wilber calls it the transpersonal levels (past and beyond the personal), where we succeed in becoming more than a person, not worried all the time about our personal problems; something we are inside of that is eternal, a place where we reside, the ultimate confidence of God, of knowing that we are more than just a body. This is a place we go and sit (be) — see the drama. But something deep inside understands we are not the drama. There is something way beyond that which appears to be real, something eternal, divine, perfect. No matter how thick the confusion, no matter how horrendous or minor the problems, they — these, it, all this "much ado about nothing" — is not us.

Something deep inside us all knows more, has a perfect place, an inner Utopia to reside in, a place we can sit fat and happy, be little doodads, find the progressing reality, the gushing forth place that is happening yet is changeless, motionless, peacefulness, realness, absoluteness, God-ness.

Even Chaucer talked of this detached point of view, of watching from a distance, to simply see, being the calmness that gets to watch from a placid seashore, being a bystander, a mere passerby who does not get involved.

It is not that we do not respond, not that we become cold fish, unemotional, not that we have no compassion, no reason left to create some slight bit of personal excitement or turmoil; rather, it is as if we go through what we go through as always, as usual, but a part of us inside is at arm's length, a part of us is not getting involved as the other parts (in some pretended way) are seemingly involved. We see the drama, the timeline, things in motion in space as simply illusions rushing by as we sit at the right hand of God, as we bask in the eternal, as we know, deeply know, will always know that we are not merely mortal but spiritual, eternal, something divine on the vine, something stupendous and great but not caught up in any proclaimed greatness: no ego, no power, no greed, no desires that can control us, enslave us any longer.

And it is a wondrous, real place to be, a place many have known about, an oasis in personal development that goes beyond pettiness of getting more stuff for ourselves, of achieving, of setting goals (and with grit and sweat get to them) to actualize something, or of becoming powerful egos who can change the world. Instead, it is a place where we can be peaceful, happy, content, living a distance from the drama that is taking place, a secure place to be where the candle cannot be blown out, the blowtorch in the hurricane is always with us. We are satisfied and find our peace in being rather than in achieving, or getting, or doing.

But we can still achieve, do, get, desire, it just doesn't have its hold on us — we don't take it so seriously. We only play because that is what linear existence is all about. We just pretend to be involved because it is better to take part in the illusion, more fun to play the game when we know, can see, understand it is, after all, merely a game. We have no commitment to win or lose, no tangible goals to make happen. We can make things happen for the sport of it, or to add a spoonful of peace to all situations, to all who seem so intensely involved. We can help them, lift them up as we play, because it is not so massively important to us anymore. Thus, we can be light on our feet.

Residing in the upper levels of existence is where we begin to believe in the Absolute, not as a concept, not as a belief taught in Sunday school, but as an actuality that we can sense and deeply know. Thus, we are, we are becoming, seem to be a long train chugging out on a vector all the way to the next galaxy, a trip of all trips where we don't even need to leave town, a place of absolute and complete security. Little can touch us, harm us, get to us; little can grab us by the balls and hurt us, make us wince; so little can worry us, detract us, throw us off the fast track, derail us; because, right here, right now, the eternal is heaven on earth, is all that we need, is us, and we are everything.

And yet, we are only bits of flesh and bone in a cosmic dance that goes on and on all night long, into the next millennium, a bag full of poetics that go well with cream cheese and fresh figs, that works well in all situations, with all people, in every country, on every planet. Finally we start to realize we are more than a body, we are more than what we have ever been taught. We find solace in the small things — the sunlight, the birds chirping in the cool spring thaw, all the old and the young, the black and the white, the perverse and normal, the lost and the found. And it all become a unified oneness.

And we don't mind. Don't mind if we are late, don't mind if the milk spills, don't mind if a seemingly good or bad situation or circumstance befalls us, because we are, and there is, a part of us that is not getting involved. This is a place so close to where we can live without pain, strife, without an attachment to what is going by us...as we just watch the eternal changing clothes, the dance, the bedazzlement of God who loves to express, mystify, invent, create, double back on us, trick Itself.

BE

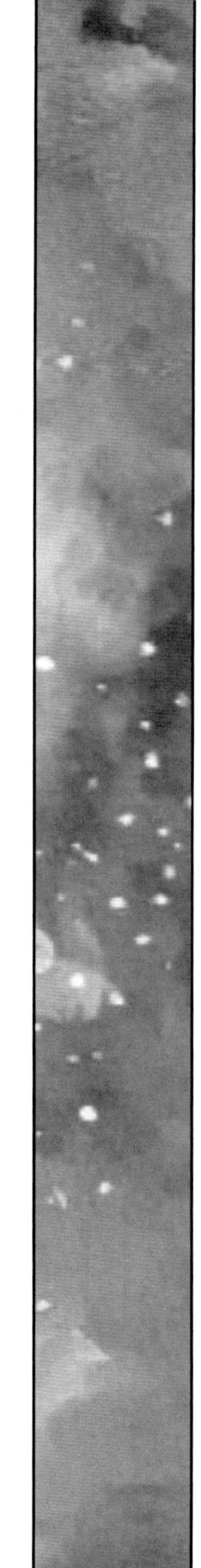

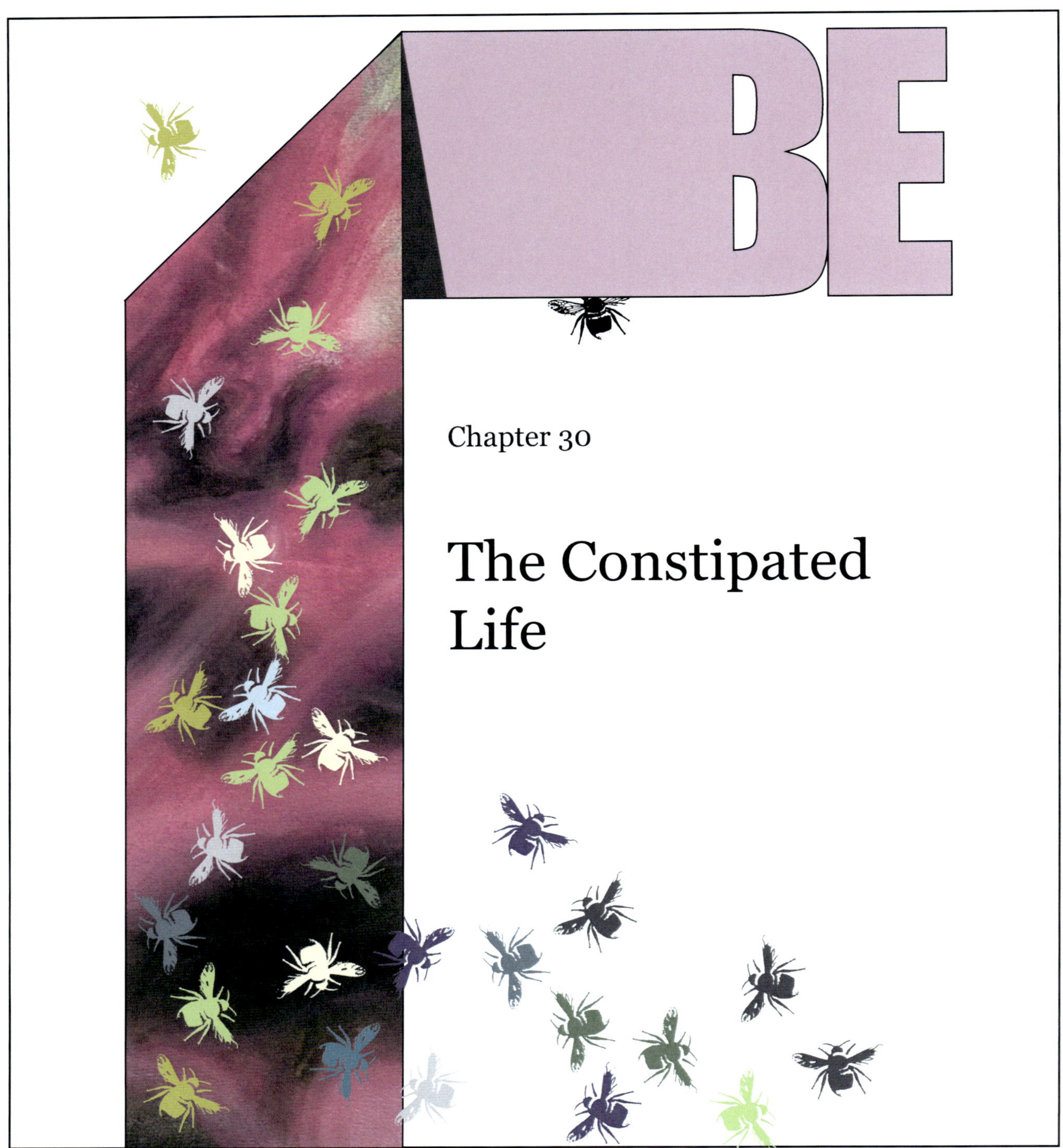

Chapter 30

The Constipated Life

Or, euphemistically put, the life of irregularity, of holding back, not feeling, of selective memory loss, of pretending that all is well in the land where the Emperor has no clothes.

We are so frightened to do what we envision ourselves to do, to be the great painter, the man who rides dog sleds in Alaska, the woman who loves the man who is her spiritual equal but she is frightened all the same and runs away. Or how about the career-oriented person who cannot lose tenure, seniority, retirement so will stay put until the life is sucked from their eyes and groin? There's all this ridiculous social convention so many cling to (no matter what) until it tears out their hearts and sinew leaving little but a shell.

We can and must and should and will find peace in our doing, that which we seem to be led to do. Our intuition guides us to simply that which we feel excited and drawn to.

So many are afraid to be as they want to be. So smoke some good pot on a starlit night as a few shooting stars slice up a normal northwestern sky, or take a full day to meander and walk through the snow fields or a spring meadow, or chase the coyote into a fox hole, or a butterfly into the surreal sky, or anything that seems to be fun, exciting, different, out of what we so often deem the norm.

And why is it that we have this fear of living? Of going toward our passion? Finding that which we love to do? Chewing up the scenery? Spreading our wings and flying over the abyss between us and the God-ness of the world, where the silver lining can be woven into tapestries of gold, where the possibilities play blackjack, where we throw the dice and the roulette wheel comes up with our number.

There is a fine line between doing and being, between walking all the way to Colorado to climb mountains and taking a bus to Chicago; a fine line between what we are and what we want to do or become.

The dilemma is that there is a fine line between nothing. It is all illusion, all made up on the spot. But we must, at times, push our patterns of living, our specialized routines, into new directions: start camps for kids, make more money to benefit a worthy cause like a trip to Paris for lunch :), like giving what we've got to a homeless shelter, like burying it in the back yard.

There is one thing we can be absolutely certain of, be it the atheist, the agnostic, the religiously inclined, the doorman, the executive, the famed, the infamous, the fallen housewife, the daughter or son, the driven husband or the single person living alone: We have one moment, to express, to dig, to find, to experience — that is the certainty. This one moment that I call eternal, that many call everlasting and the pinpoint of all possibilities, this one moment that can be directed to or from our passion, to or from the direction we believe we seek, this is the perfect gift we are given.

So many believe they are trapped, in a straitjacket that only tightens, in a routine that only ruts out deeper grooves of the same existence. Many believe so strangely that we are on some predestined trail, a conveyer belt that is taking us to some place we may not want to go to.

I say get off at the next stop. Go where you want. This is life. It can be, and actually is, an experiment, an adventure, a directionless burgeoning of time and space to form an infinite and eternal child. Be that child, but not confined by social convention. It is okay to smile in the face of disaster, to smile in the face of fortune and success, to see the natural pace and passage of time as a warm blanket, full of side roads, back roads to explore, full of potential. See life as the intricate, branch-like spreading of possibilities like nerve endings in a finger trying to touch all things.

Be not afraid to journey to the next level of perception, where death seems but a coat, where all things seem integrated, where we can go left or right or back or forward or stay still, meditate next to a gentle river, or meditate on the exhaust of the bus chug-a-lugging by. And the knowing that we can do what we choose, is the freedom we seek.

Yet, the desire to reach the end of some journey is the illusion. The desire to be more content, to find more peace, is the conundrum, because this desire is what wraps its thick fingers around us dragging us down the thorny path of our own misery. But it's our delight to walk gently upon the delights of the day, to sense the God-ness of every moment, to adjust our movement through time and focus on a goal, a result that we are not addicted to. It is our delight to be passersby in the static world of the eternal, to be watchers in the watchfulness of all things. It is and should be our delight to be able to go over there and still be here, to feel absolutely free in any direction we choose, or somehow are being taken.

We need to believe in the direction at hand that is catapulting us to some new horizon of perception, a place where sin and lust and greed and jealousy cannot touch us because we can sense these things. And yet, they have no forbidden qualities, no allure, no taboo, and we can walk through the perversity and the cleanliness, and see each as mere moments in time, parts of the sublime, opposites that create a whole.

There are no traps, only a lack of possibilities in our own heads, only confusion because of some constipated part of us that will not move, has gotten caught up inside, needs more fiber, more irritable bowel syndrome to release the blockage.

Try it. Believe it. Live it. You are absolutely free to be in this world of getting there. You are absolute flowing energy attracting itself in the gushing sea of possibilities. You are able to enact new laws, change attitudes, add kindness to the misery by simply enacting a new rule, a new way.

Go for it. Be the best. Yet flow down the river, being all along the way. See all along the way. Enjoy all along the way and still be able to use an oar, a thick paddle to help miss the rocks in the way, to go over to where the wild mint grows. Stop awhile and smell it. Grind it between two fingers and smell the entire universe in that one subtle, strong, aromatic moment.

Simply put: Go for your dreams, do what you feel drawn to do. Don't look back. The universe is on your side. And remember that being is all any of us can do to enjoy the rough or placid sea we seem to be so certainly riding upon.

Chapter 31

Circuitous

Which means indirect, roundabout. She was circuitous in her speech.

To be or not to be is not the question. To be is the answer, the only answer we shall really find. It is where we can find all the truth we'll ever need.

It seems obvious, but as with all things that are obvious, there is always an element of doubt: We are of flesh and bone, of that which will perish. We are sort of caught inside an aging process. We are frail and fragile as in relationship to the ever-changing world, but there is a part of us that is eternal, a part of us that is God, that cannot and will not perish.

This part is the part that does not get involved, the part that transcends personal dilemma, the part of us that adds love and kindness because it somehow knows, logically, universally, completely that we are God, we are spirit or soul, or made up of the stuff that will not erode, cannot be burned or destroyed. This part is what we need to address. This part is the part that breathes life, sheds death like a worn-out overcoat.

And the concept of soul (of the part of us that persists) can be applied to every religion, every mystical state. We are in this world, but not of this world. We are trying to reach the Brahma state of mind. We are that which cannot be destroyed, that which is stable — so much rock-solid stuff. It is our love, our realizing that we are them and they are us. And we must treat all things with love and compassion, with kindness, because we are being kind to ourselves.

This seems so obvious, the Golden Rule: Do unto others as you would have others do unto you, and love thy neighbor as thyself, and so on.

We can be aware of the eternalness in our own breasts, can see all the way to the river of truth by simply being, and can have faith in knowing that there is a part of all of us that will live on, recur, become part of that which we call God. There is a part of us that will find its way, its own way home and bask in the eternal, no matter what we fret about, how hard we try to find permanence, no matter how much we grasp for that which is illusion. Or better said, that which is erasable and will erode, wash away, that which can fade away, will go back to its original form of dust. We must not give importance to the illusion of impermanence; instead, we continually remind ourselves of this eternalness that we may/can/are sitting fat in, this truth that is God.

We are God. God is not a concept, not someone, something. God is all things. This is all we need to focus on each and every moment of every day in order to be secure, happy, content, placid among the turbulent seas, in order for us to swim like sharks or minnows in the eternal.

As we focus on God, we need to give up childish hopes, tenuous dreams, and we must give up the parts of ourselves that we cling to: our egos, our proclaimed certainty that this is who I am: my memories, my children, my job, my attachments to all things. We must give up that which we have been taught to be dear: our dreams, our petty desires and mesmerizing goals, reasons to get more for our unworthy causes.

And what can any of us really do but talk in circles? Circumlocutionary doggerel, dogma and doggone it, the circuitous rambling of those who know but can't say. Because it isn't something that can be said, it is a state of being...not found in a state of words.

We need to cling to that which cannot fade: God, being, this moment, the part of us that Ken Wilber would say is our I-ness, the part of us that is and has always been, the part that doesn't change, that is the real us, that is like everyone else's real them. We must cling to this I-ness that is nothing less than God-ness, the eternal part of us — the soul, the spirit. But it is probably not a separate ghost-like specter, roaming around a couple feet off the ground in some ethereal fog or in some old lady's attic, not like atoms far apart enough to walk through walls. But this eternal part is more like a part of us that we will reunite with, can reunite with; right now, in this very moment, unite to the everything, the completeness. The deeper and higher our awareness, the more we realize this absolute certainty.

It is not a concept, not something to merely admire as a novel and sultry idea, but a magnanimous ideal, a perspicacious reality so overwhelming it scares the hell out of any good and healthy ego, threatens the very mainstay part of ourselves that we believe in; but it is the womb, the mother's arms we have always missed, have wanted to get back to.

And do we not speculate why is it that we are thrown into physical bodies, separate entities trying to become a oneness again? Isn't it at least interesting why are we put through all this suffering, separation, turmoil, confusion, heartache, disease, violence? Why is it that we come from the same clay, but are made to appear so individual, so unique, so body-like and such separate entities trying to muddle our way through the ebb and flow of time and space?

As Alan Watts would venture a guess: It is God himself, wanting to surprise himself. So all the seemingly tragic events are the multiplicity, the varying sides and facets of God having fun, creating. God taking separate forms to witness the world, though briefly in accordance with some eternal notion, to witness the world as a separate thing, a separate identity.

And that is the best possible explanation I can adhere to…although still mostly speculation.

We can convolute and discredit any explanation as it is still circuitousness rambling of madmen living in a mad world. But we also can find the truth in the reality of being, in sensing the absolute in every step we take, every breath we take, in every moment of this temporary existence.

Again, it comes back to being, sensing the spring in the brisk morning, watching the sunlight creep into some new day, seeing the moment-to-moment reality masking something eternal that we can pierce by simply being, sitting in meditation, taking each and every moment as one long, forever meditation, where all security is found, where all tucked-away truth is obvious, where we can and will become the actual peace that we have so long been seeking.

There is no place to go. It is as It is: God is our truth, as is everything, right here, right now, so easy to get to if we just quit trying to find it…thus, it will find us.

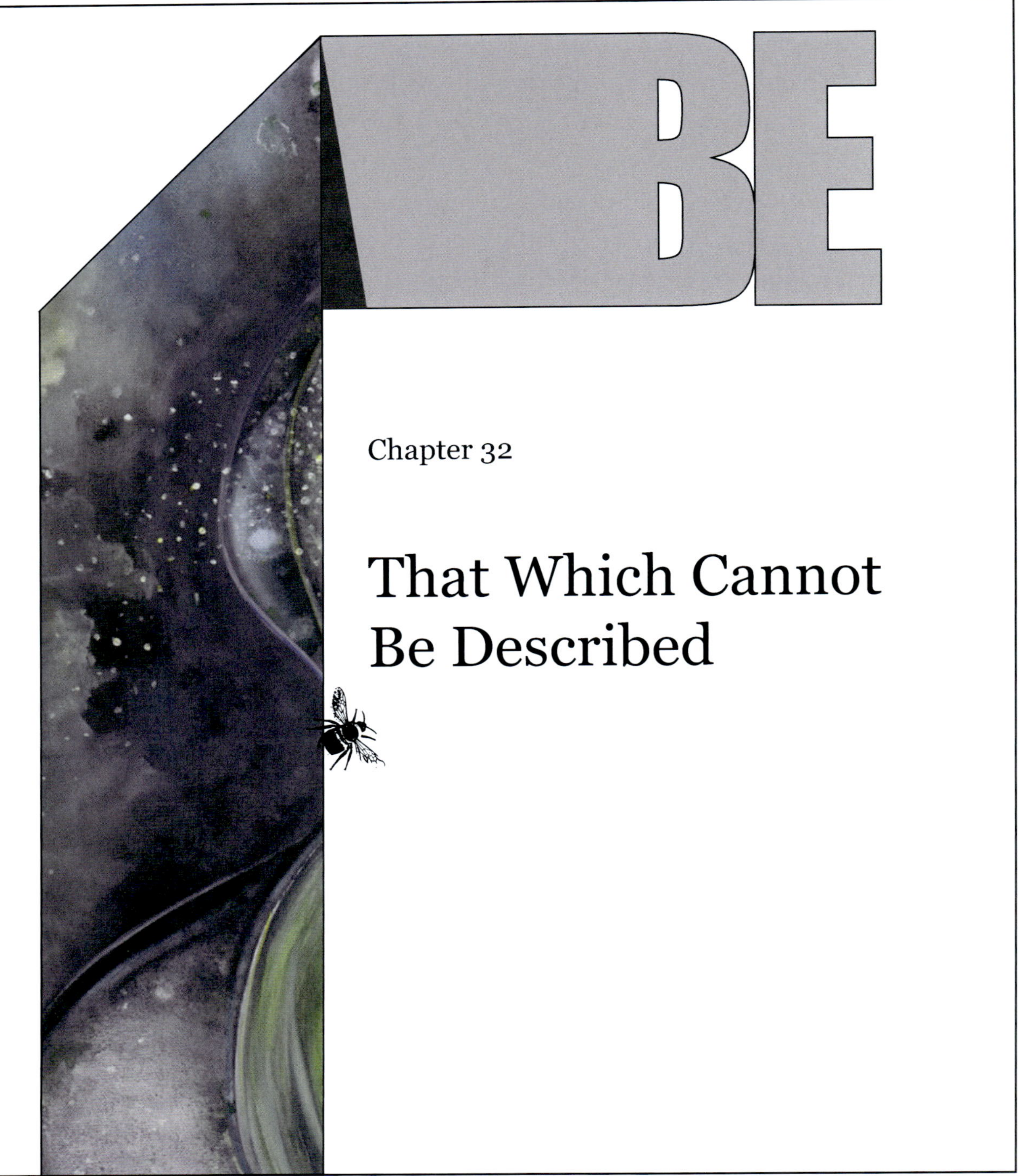

Chapter 32

That Which Cannot Be Described

There is a level of awareness that cannot be talked about, cannot be described, only pointed at, only hinted at, unless, unless you've touched upon it. Then it all makes sense. And there is no need to further explain that which you have seen, have become, the tailcoats of God, the reality of heaven on earth. It's like the oneness that you get to when on peyote, without peyote, the state of being that is so static, so completely secure that there is no need, no possibility of explanation. So why do we try, why even allude to something that has no place in the word world, has no way to be unclothed, found out, gotten to?

Well, it is a human condition to describe, to inform, to unravel, even when it is not possible.

The best way to talk of something that cannot be talked of, to try and explain the inexplicable is to first say: It is so!

I think we all get glimpses of it on moonlit nights, when a spring snow falls gently as the sun filters through a partly cloudy day, or maybe as a train whistle blows far away in the night, or when there is complete satisfaction, a wondrous day, a moment in time yet lost out of time, a touching of eternity with one hand and one foot and the rest of us is trembling behind.

I guess the best thing to do is to realize there is a state of being that transcends all others. It is a state of such blissfulness, of such suchness, of being there but not able to figure out how we got there. For there is no path to attain this enlightenment. For it is always with us, like God carrying us in the Footprint poem, like a security that goes so far beyond money, fame, loved ones, so far beyond any false sense of freedom, fading security, or ephemeral states that slip away like fish off line, like that last piece of banana cream pie snatched away at a table of a family of eleven, like all things we try to create any kind of permanence with.

In the state of enlightenment, cosmic consciousness, there are no problems, just a going though; no getting there, just an awe at being. There is no desire to find something, because all that we have ever looked for is holding our hands. There is no suffering or strife, just beauty and radiance.

And can we not be here always? Some surely are, some have been there so many times it's like second nature, while some have merely touched upon it in satori, in brief insights, some have gone to the river and drank for days and weeks and are left with the knowing and certainty that God is the ever-present security of the highest order.

If it were simple, we would all, at all times, be in this static but flowing, certain but incredible state of being. But for some reason, it is not so easy to get to, or it is so easy to get to that we make it difficult. And for those who have never attained these illustrious and iridescent states of being, all we can do is talk in seeming rhyme, riddle with a laughing fiddle, splatter paint all over something that was already strange graffiti on a night train zooming through another seedy part of town.

But we need to try and explain It, so as to know, give hope, assure us. It is important to remind ourselves that there is some place that transcends normal perception, a place of wine and roses, of beauty beyond anything we can ever write about, ever imagine. A beauty of God himself, being herself, finding it just might be an itself, and still not even caring what explanation we attach to it, because what it is, is what it is.

The goal of every human being should be to rest in this everlasting state of peace, this security that can cure all that ails us, this quiet place where humor is continuous, we can smile at the smallest of things, see through and beyond the trivial pursuits of our dear members of this race of humans.

This should be the goal of all, yet can never be a goal because a goal means something in the future. And there is no future here. Not in cosmic consciousness, only momentary insanity of the highest magnitude of sane men with lists of reasons to sit, with poetry to spew to just be spewing, with fences to fix, an inner completeness that cannot be talked of. And, yet, as we try to talk of it, we appear to be madmen in some kind of persuasive insanity infecting the masses for the purpose of undermining all social order, some innocuous pursuit of illumination that could be, from the outside looking in, a rambling of some blither on some balderdash, non sequitur lily pads of stilted awareness.

See! There is nothing that can be gotten by talking about it, only a pointing to, direction signs put up that don't even lead there, a guffawing in the face of something serious.

So where do we go from here — chasing our pursuits of the highest order, of seeing God, of being God, of witnessing the undulating reality perform its shimmering dance?

That is the point — there is nowhere to get to, all is with us. The ship is already on the cruise. The journey has begun and ended and is forever, all at the same time — you choose.

But please believe, no matter how much hot air you think is tucked between these words of light folly, no matter how far off the mark you perceive these words to be, if what is being said seems too simple, vapid, or life just doesn't seem that it can be so basic, at least believe one absolute, incredible, truth: It, God, the All is with you, me, us, right now. There is no other true truth in the expanse of this infinity we are caught in; maybe, better said, we are placed ever so gently in like a child's stick-boat on a mountain pond. It helps to always remind ourselves of this, continuously, so as to sneak a peek, slip into it, become that which we know so wonderfully and completely and absolutely... is.

BE

Chapter 33

Spiritual Revolution

Many believe as we are at this millennium, as the problems of the world are so "in your face" with the global media coverage, that we are experiencing a spiritual rebirth, a kind of revolution.

And this is as debatable as any other seemingly relevant concept of the day because so many of the great mystics have known of the oneness, of enlightenment, of higher awareness, of the folly of the 10,000 Things, and so on. And it could very well be that with the advent of books and computers there is a freer flow of information, a more accepted view that we can get to these wondrous states. And many seem to be searching in dark, basement-like metaphysical bookstores, on late night public radio stations airing Alan Watts. But, as I said before, we do not need another Jesus, or another Buddha, or another Lao Tzu, Chang Tzu, Mohammad. We need a million of these enlightened beings to change the state of affairs, to turn greed back from the gates of indulgence, to realize everything we do has an effect on everything else, and as we take, we interrupt and destroy, and as we live in lower states of consciousness, we damage, hinder, hurt, hold back that which is going to manifest anyway.

We have a perennial, social, religious, absolute obligation to uncover/discover that within which can bloom: the blissfulness, the rapture, the radiance of living. Then we can share it with others. We need to work together to form a union of spiritual developments, not to draw lines in the sand between you and me, this and that, between big business and small business, between my agenda and yours.

We need to accept that we can and will find harmony in sharing, in working together, in adding peace to a situation, in accomplishing things that involve a certain kind of shared involvement. Not because of some serious, determined mission we are on to change the world, but because if we begin to emphasize the spiritual, then the spiritual will unfold for all of us. And then we can see the effect of love on coming together, on growing things, on illuminating darkness that seems to creep into the corroded edges of bad intention, of impure motives, of the getting more for the self that (as many have said over and over) does not even exist — not as we perceive it.

Collaboration, cooperation, giving, serving, organizing things that will uplift, that will inspire, things that will add too instead of take away. These are our steps toward a spiritual revolution if it is to come, become, arrive, if we are to grow massively in awareness as a people, and see that we can and are of one God, one world, one universe, one moment. And the rest is really mudslinging on some white-shirt Sunday. The rest is merely a way to complain because we are not brave enough, wise enough, courageous enough to smile at the confusion and begin to clear up the mess, create something wonderful, envision a reality with a wondrous benefit to and for the many.

Probably the only spiritual revolution we are seeing is a deep understanding by many that we need to do something, change paths, tack, go different directions, tweak something unsettling inside, an inner conflict. And then (once that is settled) we can look behind and beyond convention to see through the illusions, the constraints, the convolution of too many misaligned things interwoven into ourselves. So many only want something for themselves, and the hell with the rest of us. Too many are on the inertia ride, not wanting to go another direction because, well, this direction is known, fine, because, well, "I've been going this way for so long. I can't think of any other way to go or to do things."

And even all this highbrow talk of change and dreams in the wind and detour ways of walking down the paths of societal restraint is still talking in gibberish limericks, winding gold thread around a sacred pipe, is much ado about nothing. Because It is with us and we are It and this present moment is not only God and us watching us, not only the surging of energy through space and time, to create a single point of eternal proportions, but rather this is us. We are the energy. We are the moment. We are not watching the moment. We are not truant, on the outside. We are the very process we are trying to discover. We are part and all, divine and undivided.

So the biggest spiritual revolution is awareness: seeing, being, no fear when it comes to finding this experience of oneness. Go for it, dream but do not letting these dreams (their imagined outcomes) be a master. So we're actually able to decide and want to create (as does the creator), for we are part of the creator's imagination. We, alike, are trying to reproduce ourselves, as Alan Watts would speculate. We are trying to reproduce biologically, artistically, technologically, conceptually, and there is nothing wrong with that. We emulate the creator, because we come from, feel, want to be, are the actually process and also love the creative process...that is us.

A dear friend once said, "We are all in our own sandbox, and we need to play, discover, build, do, dream," but really it is all just a sandbox of potential and opportunity. And so some people's sandboxes are bigger than others', have more toys, more sand. But we are all in a state of play, a state of fondness for, a state of becoming, be it excited, mesmerized, delighted, but usually in the states of rapture and bliss and adoration of the gentle and incredible and distinctive and momentous beauty going on, going past. And we are that beauty, are also beautiful renditions of the ancestral fire that keeps aflame, keeps burning, and churning, and we are the very processes that we are so amazed by, the process that we witness, the universe in "a grain of sand." And we are this spiritual revolution that has been happening since the dawn of time, since the time of Confucius, Emerson or Gandhi.

Probably, there will always be those exceptional individuals who see clearly and try to explain it to all the ones with cataracts. There will always be but a handful of those who lead us through the desert into the promised land (but most really want to stay in the desert worshipping cacti and stray cows, whether they realize it or not).

There will always and only be (and maybe for good reason) but a few who can listlessly yet lightly, reside in the highest states of awareness, and can smile and point to and discuss it.

But mostly, these wondrous beings can be us, you, the man down the street, because all they do, which we probably don't do, is not resist the world of spirituality. They bask in it, find refuge there/here, are not afraid to lose the tiny self to get to the BIG SELF, aren't afraid to smile near the garbage cans in surly alleyways.

Flash freeze awareness, instant becoming, get there and stay there. Seek no more. Believe "the bottom of the bucket" can and will fall out. Sense the truth. Try on a new pair of shoes. Be willing to investigate. Drink wine in the summer on the open-air deck of some new certainty. Crawl out of the skin and begin. Become the poet with a slide rule and a bag full of chaotic mathematical equations. Run the race. Sit in the stands. Be the experience...experiencing itself. And then all things will shed the snakeskin — the illusion will be dispelled.

BE

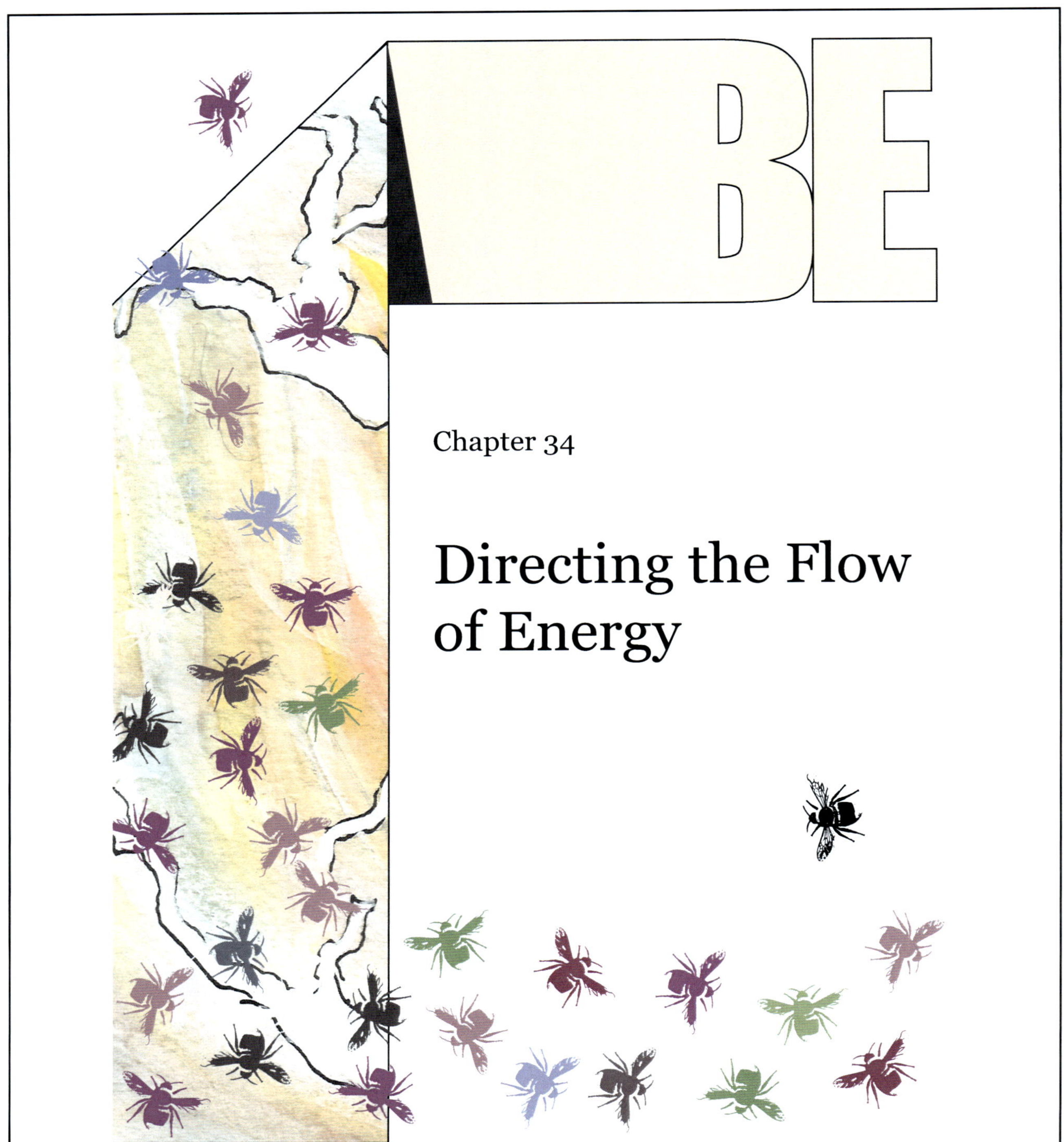

Chapter 34

Directing the Flow of Energy

The more we see ourselves as one, as the energy flowing, as the process, the allness of the All-ness, then the more we can direct the flow of energy toward the common good, toward the benefit of the all. Because as we serve, help each other, then we are actually helping ourselves. There is no difference between me and you and them and getting more for me without giving more to It.

As we become of higher awareness, as we realize our entitled enlightenment, our God-given right to sense the eternal and to be part of that which is everlasting, as we enjoy the process and feel — deeply — that we are this process, then we want to serve, to give back, to begin to add to the overall good, for one reason: It's us anyway.

Maybe we should value other things: slipping through a new day, watching the geese on the still pond, wanting to sit by the river. For then our energy is, will be, of a helping nature, wanting to give more, serve the common good instead of raping the land, instead of seeing how much we can stuff in a mattress and save for later.

What is it we should value? Should we be able to get all that we want? Drive the fanciest of cars? Finance a castle and fly our helicopter to and from work? Should we create wealth unmatched because we can, or should we live as Gandhi did: loin cloth and a bowl of rice? (Live simply so others can simply live)?

It is a choice. If we believe we can accomplish more by owning a plane, own a plane. If our motives are pure (which is sometimes a hard thing to accurately determine), and if we seem to have the need to gather and amass large reservoirs of money, and we do not become defiled, tainted, distorted by the glitter and power of these false pursuits, then it must be okay.

However, all that is outward, all that we believe we need, be it more money, more recognition, more love, more sex, whatever it may be, therein lies the illusion. The more we are pulled from the present moment, looking, peering into a false crystal-ball future, the more we are drawn toward the carrot on the stick, dangling in front of us as we run like wild dogs in a 'round and 'round race. The more we do this, surely the more we are off-track.

Whatever we do, as long as we understand it is a game, merely ways to entertain ourselves as we sunbathe in the forever, in the eternal moment, then all is well in the land of the Oz we create. And as we sit securely in the present, we will want to enjoy it, add to its snakeskin nature of shedding, of changing, because, what it does...we do, we are also.

When we find new games to play, experience what we want because it is our chance as separate consciousnesses, then the world is our oyster, a playground of discovery, possibility, latent potential waiting around for us. So then we do what we do, not because of the reward (or the result, or the meaning, or the purpose of it), but because it is fun and exciting, gives us reasons to persist in this illusion, ways to surprise ourselves.

The key is to be as we strive for our important endeavors, as we create the game, as we watch how we can use energy and inertia and dreams to create, manifest. And eventually, we get more people to work together so that they will all get something, add something, help initiate a change that may — we hope — seem to be illustrious, shimmering, God-guided, an incredible completeness of all things working to create a more perfect union, a common bond. This brings out people's genuine goodness, thus helps them help each other so all can feel, sense, be the bond that we so often avoid. Thus, we realize we are droplets in the river of change, fathers to all, markers on the trail of discovery and awe.

BE

Chapter 35

Be Careful of Having to be Right

We should all have a healthy dose of contempt for our precious ideas, our verification of what reality is, how the world fits together in our brains.

As once seen on a bumper sticker: "Don't believe everything you think."

Of course, I mentioned the girl who saw (and I'm sure still sees) fairies, creatures in the trees, naked, glorious and shimmering with wings, flying through the air or perched on a lone branch, and I must say, I must leap, jump across the chasm, suspend my disbelief. Why? Are there strange creatures at the bottom of the sea with lights on their heads, or giraffes with long necks and giant yellow patches on them? Are there probabilities in quantum mechanics, massive amounts of uncertainty, aliens visiting? Then why can't there be fairies in the trees?

But this is not the issue, for the issue is that there is enlightenment. There can so very easily be a spiritual awakening. It happens. There are people who are so advanced, so suspended in eternity, whatever you want to call it — those of higher awareness, spiritual beings wandering the hills and streets of this earth — who are just as unbelievable as fairies in the trees. And most don't care, most simply want to be right. Most don't want to become, attain, find, slip into enlightenment. They would rather be right, drunk with their own righteousness, clinging to their religions, to their stubbornness, sitting content in some kind of mock contentment in a certainty that is worse than fairies in the trees. So many see life as only this way and no one (no enlightened being, no wise guy) is going to tell them any differently.

This is a trap with sharp teeth for all of us who are trying to maintain our inner peace, who are trying to see further and farther into and out of the illusions that bind us. We get so much resistance from those who think they know, from those who see only black and white in a multicolored, multifaceted world. And we cannot get through the walls they have built up around themselves to justify their lives, rationalize the way they live, the security they have sold out for, the valueless things that they so certainly must defend.

So the point: Beware of the righteous, the doomsdayers, the ones who have it all figured out. And yet what seems so amusing is that when we look in on their misery and suffering, they don't seem like they've figured it out quite right. These are the ones who draw lines in the sand, the critics: the legless men teaching running. Critics are those who put you here and them over there, put ideas in boxes, shove their certainty, their own brand of certainty, on the rest of us because they know it all, and they are too afraid to have uncertainty as part of their arsenal of light weapons to attack the world.

All I am saying is that what I have written is real, at least possible, but has room to be amended, has breathing room to be expanded, can be seen more clearly by beings more astute and advanced than I.

So instead of ideas, concepts, fairies in the trees or righteousness with a gross and sticky film all over it, trust in experience, in the moment, what actual spiritual revelations you create from within, and be so very careful of OPOs (other people's opinions).

We are continually discovering, wondering, finding out, reaching for the stars, visualizing perfection in the passing of what we call time.

I have always believed that reality is malleable, soft clay to be molded, and that reality is negotiable. No one has the pat answer to it, and that reality is more of an accommodation; it accommodates our perception, reinforces what we believe, and anything we believe in hard enough is never very hard to believe. For as we believe, we see that reality. There will always be an element of truth to this.

We have a limited view of the world, and our conceptual reality will always be incomplete, but this is as it applies to the change, the flux that we see going by, the thought process itself.

Now, from pure experience, I know there is something that is static, unchanging, eternal beneath the river of change and time: Call it God, truth, the infinite and the eternal commingling to form a reassurance, the ultimate inner security. This, for me, has no room for compromise. This can be touched upon in actuality, not as a possible actuality, but as a complete and fulfilling experience. Anything that is a concept (any debatable idea) can be whittled away, chopped up. But the actuality of this moment as eternal can also be a concept. And when taken inside, when felt, when the satori hits, the deep insights unfold, and knowing that all the sages of the world have talked of this similar experience in the similar ways, then there is an ultimate reality and truth to it. And it can be settling, real, but never limited in its way of wanting to convince, to make others believe it is real. It is only an actuality that is soft, caring, gentle, and It can understand and comprehend the fear and fringes of others trying to refute its realness.

So on our journeys in and out of these states of higher consciousness, remember there is a God, a reality, a blanket to keep us warm. There are realities untold, imaginations beyond comprehension. But there is also something so real we can all touch upon it, this instant, this instant, this...instantaneous epiphany.

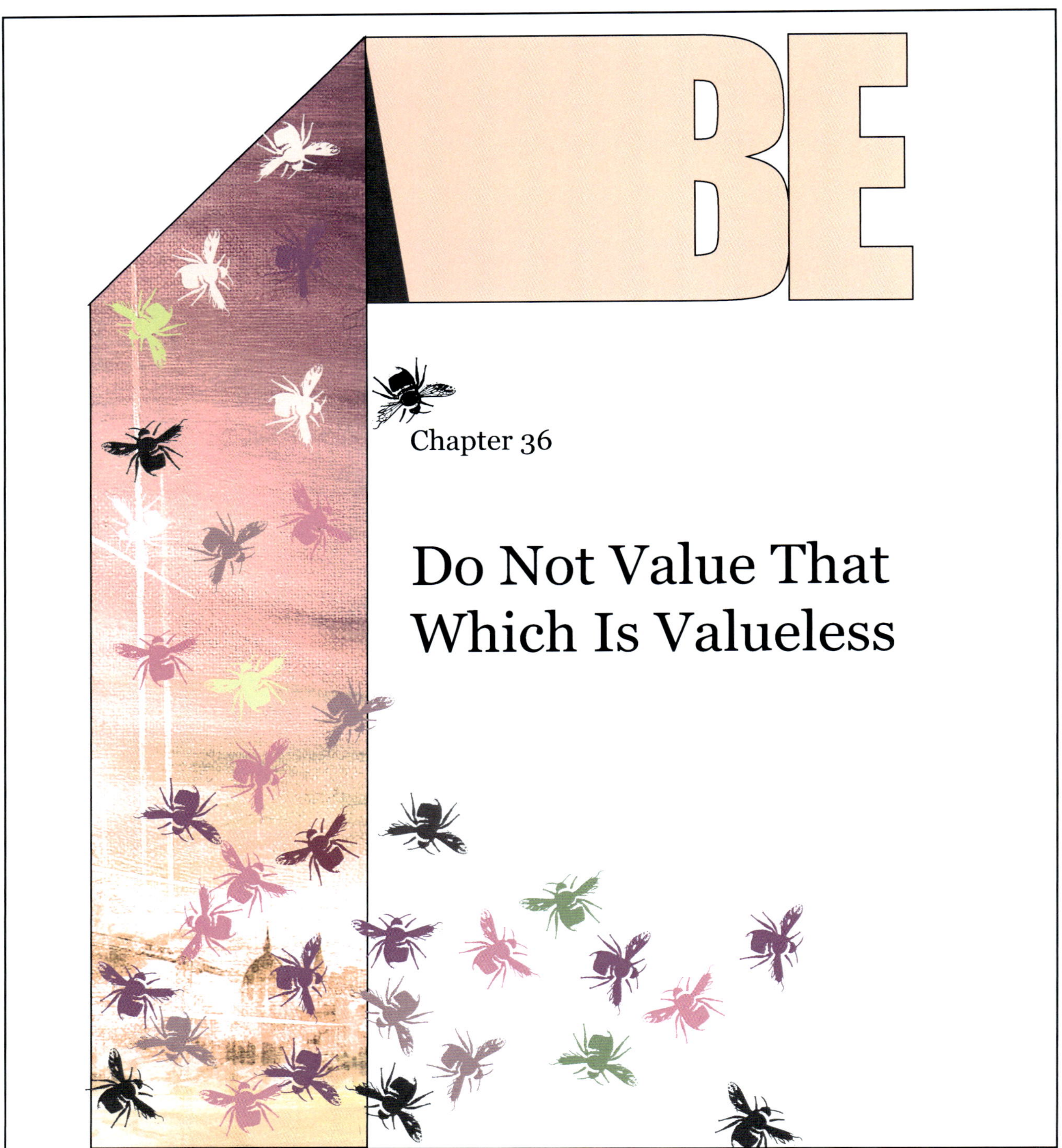

Chapter 36

Do Not Value That Which Is Valueless

If we are searching for our enlightenment, finding it in the chattering of the squirrels, finding it in the scintillating moments of right now, seeing truth in the quivering aspen leaves rustled by a soft mountain breeze, or in the dandelions sprouting in the grass as spring is greening the hills...then we will value that which is eternal.

But why is it that others value such nonsense and get so lost in the pursuits of things, money, prestige, lost in their goals of getting more, having more? And for what purpose?

We should value the time we have with each other, the ones who we love, value those things that spur us on to help and serve the greater good, to benefit the most.

We must value the passing moment no matter what form it takes, be it work, morning coffee, vacation time, mowing the lawn, doing taxes — it is of the same stuff, same mud, same nourishment that can feed us.

So many want to get things: new houses, new cars, digital phones, computers, want so intently to live a standard of living portrayed in the movies, in commercials. So many want to have the perfect family like in the Brady Bunch...but the father, in reality, died of aids. Just remember, Jesus rode upon a donkey and had one pair of sandals, no summer home on the Florida Coast. And Jesus didn't hang out with prestigious and powerful people, more like fishermen and carpenters and poor people.

So many think the perfect life is one of narrowing, limiting our neuroses, with waning amounts of emotionally bloated overreacting, filled with feelings of jealousy when a neighbor has more, gets a new car, feelings of fear in our judgment of others. Although these reactions may have their place, we should let them go quickly.

Tara Singh says, "These things we feel, things that bother us, will not last long if we do not oppose them."

Do not oppose the uncomfortable thoughts and feelings, then uncomfortable thoughts will disperse like new morning fog on the dirt road of tomorrow, will fade right into black.

But what is it that we seem to chase that is valueless, and why, in heaven's name, in the name of the Father, in the name of sanity, why do we chase these temporary things (call it the elusive future) that fade and become dust?

Society claims to make us value these things: the good job in a big corporation, a title, a prestigious seat on some intellectual panel, the house with the picket fence, the IRAs and secure retirement plans for those with most of the life sucked out of them by the age they get to collect these things they've so long been waiting for anyway because they bought into these social values that quell inspiration and peace of mind, that block and stem the tide of the divine.

If we have been mostly poor our entirely lives, of course we may be drawn to wealth. It has a "never been there, never had it" allure. So we get our wealth and hopefully lose it and see it as an impostor in the ritual of deceit.

We may value education, get real educated, lots of fat letters behind our name, and maybe, if we are perceptive, will outgrow our titles and distinctions, then just be an average Joe with inner peace and contentment.

The biggest problem in this life is that so many value that which is valueless, that which will not persist in the fire of truth, that which can bring no peace.

As I have said it before, all anyone really wants in their life is peace, contentment, radiance, lasting bliss, rapture, to be happy most of the time. And when we value that which is external, that which cannot give us our peace, then we are on some treadmill of thinking we are getting somewhere. But we will never arrive — like a tiger chasing its own tail that it will never catch, like living for tomorrow instead of for right now, this day, today. It's like believing someday, some glorious day, we will be in heaven, thus we lose the spirit of the moment, the enjoyment of the present which has the key to all that we could ever conceive we want and need.

Valuing that which is valueless is sin in the religious way of looking at it.

But what is it we should value? Giving, sharing, creating something of beauty: be it a painting, a new piece on the piano, a business that may help all involved, a poem, a book, a stable home for our small, delicate and fragile children. Or it could be that we should value the moment of what is happening right now (because all the philosophy and mental machinations will never be as complete as what is happening right now) and then we will respond accordingly with gratitude and love.

It is all about helping and serving, to value giving, to value adding a spoonful of peace to every situational comedy we find ourselves involved in, to see through the games people are playing, but to let them play the game of their choice until it loses its appeal, loses its priority. For we cannot help those who do not wish to help themselves or dispel the myth of what they value until the myth dispels itself and the fog lifts.

Those drawn to addictions, or distractions, or more and more money or status must find their own ways through to the other side of these ephemeral pursuits. And not until they have sucked the marrow from these endeavors will they be ready to move on.

But for those who are ready to value that which is eternal (God, truth, beauty, the moment), they are open to a new world, open to discovering the gold buried under the fool's gold they've been digging and scratching at. Only then will they find that which can flourish. And then the truth can grow into feathered wings and spread for all who are ready to fly.

We must value an uncluttered life, the mañana mentality found in so many third world countries. We must value our excitement to create a better world, value our friends, our loved ones, our unyielding pursuits of good and God and keep real peace in our hearts, because that is the only place it can be found, inside, in this moment, right now, near us now; not someday, or getting there, or when we arrive, or after we have that new car, or new house, or book published or sweetheart in our life to give us the tenderness we crave.

As we become enlightened beings, as we realize our true spiritual nature, nourish that part of us that is not getting involved, nurture the soul so to speak, the more we give attention to that which is eternal, then the more we naturally will value that which is true, pure, clean, vital, never-changing. And then we will find the static peace, see clearly through the games so many addictively play, and will not be bothered if someone has more than us, if someone has finer clothes, more disposable income and can fly to the Gulf of Mexico on a whim.

As we understand God is right now, heaven is right now, truth and beauty is right now, then all of the best things that we seem to be drawn to are of the present moment. And as we live day-by-day, moment-by-moment, instead of years away into some well-planned-out future, then, as John Lennon said, "Life is what happens to us as we are making plans." Experiencing life right now becomes the only and absolute reality that we can ever deeply know.

This instant is where the meat is, the universal truths, the cosmic talking to us, the Absolute putting its loving arm around our perceived problems. And then these silly problems all evaporate like a thick fog we could never see through. But now it is a clear day, it has always been, shall always be a clear day no matter how foggy the valueless reality may appear to be at first notice.

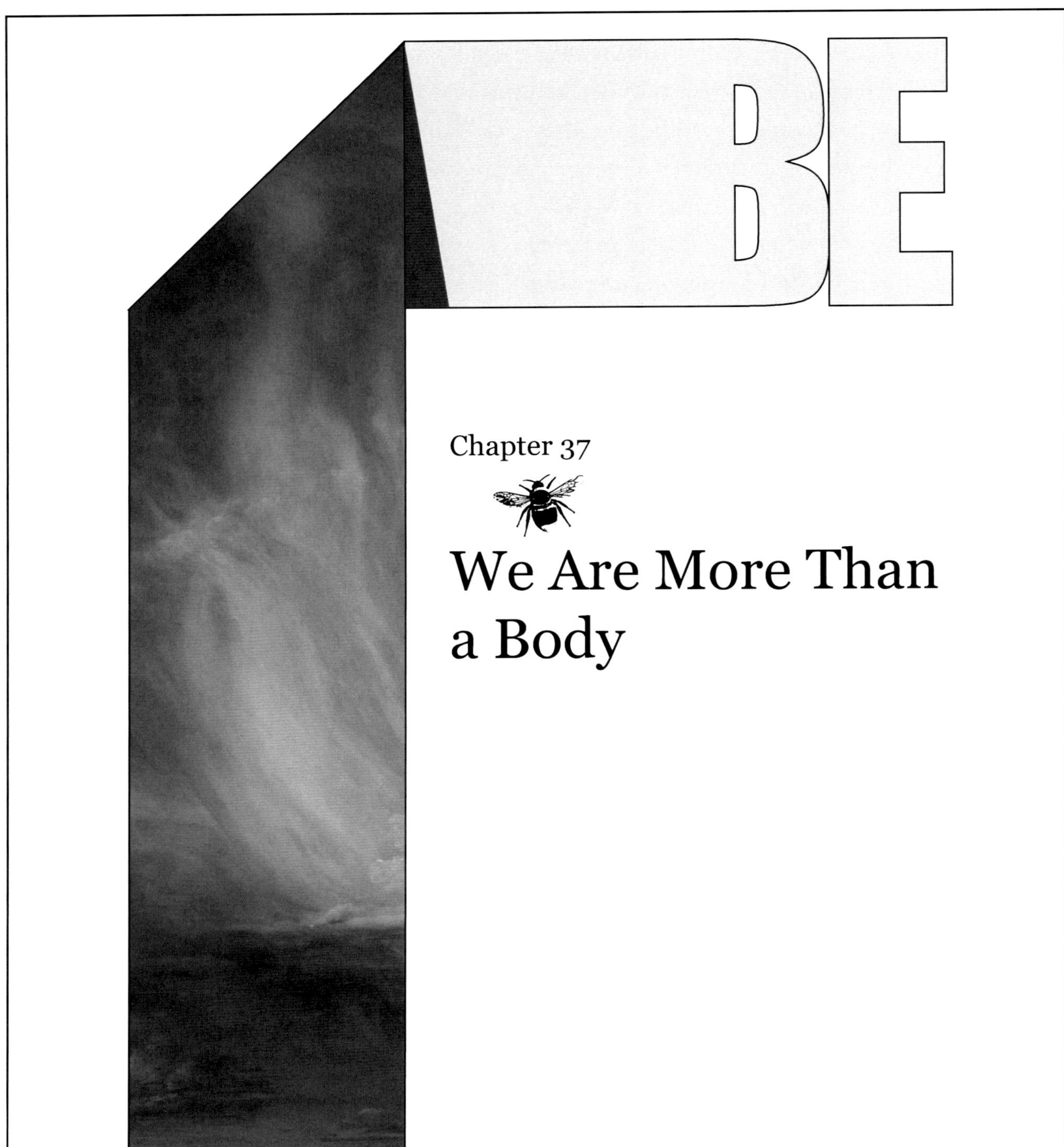

Chapter 37

We Are More Than a Body

We are a mind and a body and a spirit, and all these things are not separate things but energies, one and the same, parts of one universal spirit.

Could it be the body is us, and that we are as much body as we are anything? But we are mind, our head atop a body, as Ken Wilber likes to put it. But it is the part of us that can transcend the mind/body link, the part of us that can sit back and watch the body suffer and not be too concerned, the part of us that can witness the mind go through its protocol, think its thoughts, and still smile at the dance. And, again, it is a part of us that is doing the seeing, that is the actually outside, beyond, away from the drama we feel we are caught in.

Not that there is an outside, or a beyond, but there is an actual part of each and every person that is not emotionally involved, is not the mind, or the body, but it is there, a part that is not getting involved, a part that can be forever calm, that is connected to all things, is all things, is the drama, yet can still be detached from the drama. This is the part most refer to as soul, as spirit, as the eternal spark which is the life-force, that part which will never erode, cannot cave in on itself, a part that will survive, a part that is the I-ness, a static presentation in the churning of some kind of silver screen unreality.

How do we nurture this part of ourselves, concentrate on it, address its reality?

We are this part, more so than a body, more than a role we have been taught to believe in or to play. So to nourish this part we must first give it priority, continually be with it, sit detached with it, watch it watching, be the watching, see how it can, we can, actually become the "all things," the God-ness we have so longed for, that part of us that we pray to. It is the eternal spark in our bosoms lightly dancing, smiling, integrating all aspects of our complicated human facets and psyche that we must focus on.

As we give attention to this soul-ness part, we are magically drawn to the present, because it exists only in the present — it is the present. It cannot exist in thought, or in explanation, or diversion, or in our pursuit of socially taught priorities like goals, achievements, the excitement of some future event, or some turmoil of an unforeseen tragedy, divided by some emotional outburst. This eternal/infinite part is the rock of Gibraltar in our seemingly ephemeral lives, it is the underlying truth that connects all things, it is God in us, God being us.

So as we hold its hand, it wraps its universal arms around us, protects us, calms us, is us. And we, again, are fat and sassy reclining in the present moment, because God, this detached part of us, this part of us that is not getting involved, lives in and thrives in this eternal present moment that never ends, that is always here. And as we train and focus our minds to be, instead of thinking we must become, as we focus this part (our attention) on the here and now, we are thus basking in the eternal. We are seeing that which cannot go anywhere, can only change shapes, like chameleons in a void, can only pretend to be going in some direction, can only shoot fireworks up into the sky as if putting on some elaborate and royal display of grandeur in an attempt to elude us, maybe to entertain us, or just because this is the nature of the flux.

M. Dowling
6/18

Chapter 38

Rising Above Pain and Discomfort

Though we are a body and a body thinking, we can experience not being a body and rather experience being a motion of the hand of the eternal, gesturing. We are the world itself in all its manufactured situations, in all what seems to be moments hooked to moments hooked to other moments. But what of the body when it is in pain, gets rashes, cancer, strokes, aides, all the devastating diseases and things that can make anyone feel completely a body, a shell, a separate organism being effected? And isn't it interesting if you speak at any length with a cancer survivor, how they view their ailment, this horrible experience, as a gift?

Still, when sick, we focus on the part of us that isn't getting involved, see that we are more than the disease. We are the part that cannot be affected. And we can heal ourselves by looking for the cause, by proper treatment, by simply being, and letting this being take over. And could it be that if we continually lived in the present (peaceful, blissful) that we could've averted much of what has been attracted to us by being out of control, stressful, out of sync, harboring bitterness or hatred?

We break our leg, get cuts, canker sores, chronic body sicknesses that we cannot shake, and what are the purposes of these ailments? What can they bring to our spirituality? Maybe a humbling that we are not invincible. Maybe that we get to sense the pain, the other side, the far side, of pleasure. We get to feel in our guts the wrenching pain of a body telling us that we are in this vessel and this vessel will let us sense the world, feel the world, have the opportunity to feel pain and discomfort so as to help us reside in, come back to the eternal present. Afflictions help us stay here and not run, let us cure ourselves, or recover, or slip away into the night.

We can rise above any pain, any dysfunctionality of the body, by not running from the pain, or simply seeking proper medical attention, but also by believing their is cure to all illness. Or as one woman I once met, a healer, said (or what she said an angel who had visited her in the night had told her): "Heal the heart and you heal all things."

And if we can make it through the course of our disease, we can come away with something that is of a knowing nature, be it compassion for others in similar situations, be it a deeper love for those who are suffering, or simply a way to distance ourselves from ourselves to become more than we could ever believe: an essence, a transcendence, thus spiritually able to overcome, heal, step away from the pain.

The body is where we get to have sensation, pleasant or vile, and it is the temple where we have the opportunity to sense the eternal by actually being separate, by being a moment of consciousness riding the wave of foreverness. This is opportunity. This is bliss even in painful situations. This is a gift from God to God, from Himself to Himself, from the world back to the world.

We can rise above and beyond illness if we choose to, if we are not ready to let go of the body and drift back home; or, if we desire, we can heal ourselves to get through our pain and suffering.

Again, it is the present that holds the key to rising above the pain, to find that part of ourselves that is protected, is forever, that cannot be hurt, cannot listlessly expire with the physical body that we have so long identified with.

So if there is some illness that has you in its grip, think healing thoughts, believe in the body's incredible built-in ability to heal itself and let all modern medicine try its stab at it, but use thought to aid all cures, the peaceful thoughts of the body's magical ability to regenerate health and become stable and balanced.

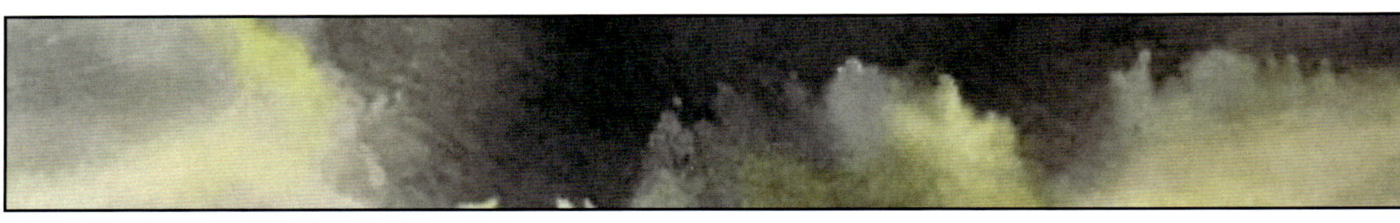

BE

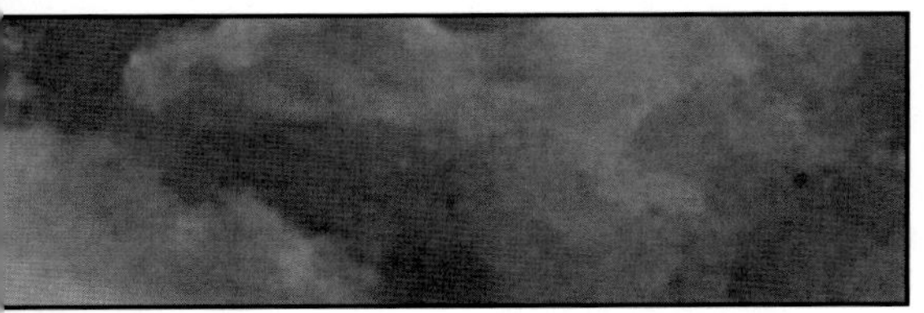

Chapter 39

Traveling the Universe

Recently we, they, someone has discovered planets in newly discovered solar systems with elliptical orbits that maybe even cross like two planets intersecting yet orbiting around the same star. They have also found some planets 10 times the size of Jupiter, some with sulfuric or some such atmospheres, also cosmic thunderstorms. What can this tell us or point to? In what amazing sailboat do we find ourselves? What amazing things exist beyond the most fertile imagination of the sci-fi writer? Arthur Clarke is alive and well.

If only we had the vehicle or the know-how (but Einstein made light-travel so heavy) then we could travel millions of light years, parsecs upon parsecs into the outer reaches of the universe and still get nowhere, and how could this be?

It's like being a ham radio operator in the 1950s, out in the ether picking up signals from somewhere, maybe Indiana, Russia, or from Orson Welles.

What is so amazing is that we actually are able to plug into the essence of the universe right here, right now, like setting our watches to Kant as he did his daily walk (it was said he never left his hometown, didn't go more than 30 miles away, yet had a view of the world of the best-traveled).

We can travel the universe, or travel in books, or ride the telescopic light to distant planets. But easier still, we can travel to the farthest reaches of this undulating foreverness by simply being, tapping into the universal energy, witnessing the flux that is happening on the fringes of some proverbial edge of the known universe. And we can feel the power of the eternal present simply by sitting on the back porch and gazing up to the heavens and not thinking how far that star is, not analyzing the molecular structure of anything, but rather by being computer illiterate, irrationally logical, by sensing the earth's rotation, the completeness of everything in the right now going 'round and 'round.

Many will not believe in anything that they cannot see or touch, so I say, "Carry around a microscope." But still that doesn't get us to the core, just to more parts, smaller and smaller parts.

Or maybe like in astronomy or astrophysics, we can get to bigger and bigger parts and pictures of the universe, more amazing stories of gravitons, tiny black holes covering the face of the infinite, quasars larger than our solar system, comets coming back around every 4,000 years or so...and what does it even mean? Where does it get us? Into the atom or out there on some fantastic mental voyage? Maybe it gets us to tremble at the magnificence of this mysterious world, gets us into the imagination of a universe so macro and yet so micro, so define-less, so perplexing, so more and above our tiny little troubles that we certainly believe to be important as we drive down a paved street on some dull day wondering if our tax check came in yet.

But we are more than this. We are the actual edge of the universe. We are the imagining of the greatest minds dreaming up sci-fi creatures that resemble tire treads with ear holes and black-dot eyes. We are larger than the concepts that we create, thicker than the hair on black holes, as incredible as the light taking us to the moon on a harvest autumn evening. We are the possibilities forming, the intrigue of new discoveries. We are the darkness and dark matter between unknown galaxies rubbing elbows... for we are the universe itself.

We don't have to go anywhere, not in a spaceship (unless we get a good deal on cheap tickets), don't need to go anywhere in imaginary thought, don't need to leave home, don't need to go anywhere, because the universe comes to us, it is us. We can tap into its beauty, its source, its mystical qualities just by being.

We can travel the entire scope of this vast universe by letting the universe become us, by realizing that we are everything in every place, on every planet, in all sectors, and it is as magical as flying through the air at 40,000 miles per hour behind some comet with handbags packed, as mystifying as riding shotgun with Arthur Clarke in the year 3001 as he espouses his new conceptual reality of what might and could be as we zoom down a dirt path in his four-wheel something or other chasing iridescent, purple Bengal tigers in the jungles of what once was Sri Lanka.

Travel wherever you want, but the greatest trip is to become the universe right here, right now, forever, and tap into the energy of all things — the ultimate trip of enlightenment.

M. DOWLING 6/18

Chapter 40

Stopping the Snow

And what is it that is so important? What is it that we fret about? What is it that we get in a frenzy about? And after all, after we've put ourselves through the entangled world of worry and fret, after we have run the gamut of emotions (either suppressed, or resisted, or tripping over these emotions), what then? Doesn't the world still exist, the universe still become, the gentle flow still actually be... gentle flow?

There are no problems, just a perception that there are problems, just a resistance to change, just a fear of a future that has not yet arrived or something we concern ourselves with that is stuck in the past that is long gone.

Action should be based upon a flow, a watching what is happening and seeing the potential of that moment. Action should be administered like an inoculation, to help, an adding to, a clarity rather than a blur of things to be done or a whirl of crazed motion charging through space.

There is an ever-present security, a getting there by being there, a non-resistance to what is happening out there and in here, an uplifting of what we deem necessary to a preference, a desire to bask gently in eternity rather than to charge forward into the bright future of "someday."

So often we run around trying to get there, to organize everything so well that there is no place for error, no place for the ooze to seep out, no place for spontaneity. And we believe we actually can control reality, we can make things better, believe we can abort tragedy before it happens; we can protect ourselves from what may be lurking around the corner, what may be stalking our organized world of perfection.

We cannot organize reality. We flow with it, add to it, nudge it, love with it, give to it, react less to its challenges, ask the right questions of our perceptions, be kind to life's twists and turns, but we cannot control it. We can merge with it, maybe act upon it, invent a portion of it, but we cannot prevent it. And sometimes we just need to let things go, not be so absorbed in an outcome of "how come?" or a desired result.

But shouldn't we rather be enveloped in the mystery of not knowing, in the fringes of reality, in the heavy fog of a dream-like state that is a perplexity all unto itself, and (at times) accept that which is not always complete clarity? We should almost worship that which is enigmatic, smile at the subterfuge, the intrigue, yet fear not, but have faith in the calm, placid truth of a still mystery that is slipping away and coming to us, that is here today and...here today and still here...today. That is the simplicity, the wonder, the small parts of awe and rapture that commingle together to form an aspect of beauty.

Sometimes we just need to let go of the control we think we have over reality, and, in reality... just be. And then we can just merge with that being, see windows open because we're looking for the open doors, because they are there, because we see, watch, are not running after abstract thought, but being, merging into the clean purity of NOW, a kind of materialism, of concrete truth, all that is smiling next to us in this theater of the absurd, in this play of beauty and truth and good stuff juxtaposed next to that which scares the hell out of a part of us.

Letting go of things that we cannot control, being less addicted to what we have been taught is important, and just simply being, adding peace, creating a security of presence, this is as important as building the greatest of bridges. This is as amazing as having erected the Great Wall of China, as impressive as creating a spaceship that can fly all the way to Pluto and take pictures of a tiny sun.

BE

Chapter 41

Stopping the Snow #2

It is April 24th. It started snowing and it kept snowing all day, and it rose up to around two feet in 24 hours.

In Colorado these things happen. Some became agitated, like it was a long-enough winter, some were elated, some didn't care at all.

Many wanted to stop the snow. You cannot stop the s-now! Life is more of a melting rather than an about-face, more like a mellowing than a changing of the world.

All that we need is in the NOW, in the moment. And all that we desire, all that we are frantic about is possible to redirect, is possible to watch with egolessness.

But many want to turn the river to run through town, as they build a new bridge put up by the city planners. Yet what toll on the self will this take?

Should we not realize the most important thing we can do is give in small amounts, add modicums of peace, a pinch of bliss, a sprinkle of the good stuff, a splash of pure delight? Then by doing this we recreate time with a merging into a state of rapture.

So many don't even know they are hurting others, are too blunt, too obtuse to see the negative energy that they spin off in all directions. And, at times, the ones who feel the hurt are usually the ones who are so hyper-sensitive, almost love to wear their sensitivity like a badge of honor.

Wouldn't it be much better if we realized our effects on others, tried to understand how we instigate turmoil without even seeing the effect we are having on our already wavering mankind? Man be kind. Woman be kind. All be kind. Else it is really a human race of no avail with no winners, a scimitar in the mouth of some dastardly and crawling guerrilla on a jungle mission, lost in the Gobi Desert.

If only we can add some peace, be peaceful, make that our goal, instead of being on some frantic mission to change the world, instead of stroking our egos more and more, with more and more education, more and more wealth, more and more civic duty and feigned applause that eventually will be quieted, all this will turn to dust like all the bridges we build.

You see there is no one to convince about our spirituality but ourselves, no one will listen because most are too hard-pressed to become someone else, to be convinced of their own Tightness. Most are full of themselves, trying to arrive somewhere, to get that promotion, trying to change the world because there is something actually inside themselves they need to change, be it a slight shift or a big kick, a tweak of inner peace, a change of attitude.

If we have a plan, a vision, a dream and want to attain it, want to let it unravel in the potential of its own possibilities, let it come into existence like a long song and a short prayer rather than like a bulldozer making it happen at all costs. If we care not so much for the result as the experience of it unfolding like a warm blanket, then...we arrive, and we create from the state of the creative mind.

But if we have a vision of how things should be, how to make the world correct/right, how to show those idiots who definitely don't understand how to understand, then this may not be the right path to follow, the right seed to sow, the right sow's ear to be chewing on.

Peace should always be our goal. Love should always be our settledness. Watching the effect we have on others, minimizing the effect we let them have on us, should be our highest awareness.

We may not be able change the world, but we can change our perception of how the world is. We cannot see through the illusion until we stop being the illusion, stop wanting to be part of the illusion. We cannot make a difference until we are the difference in motion.

Add peace, and the world will come into alignment all by itself. Be gentle, and the rest of us in the world will learn that gentleness. Be the example, smile at the drama others get caught in. And then, that which we deem so important instantly becomes sliced watermelon on a hot day, becomes a soft rain on the small bonfire, becomes a beautiful snowstorm that we don't even want to stop.

Better than cooking on a hot day, I suppose.

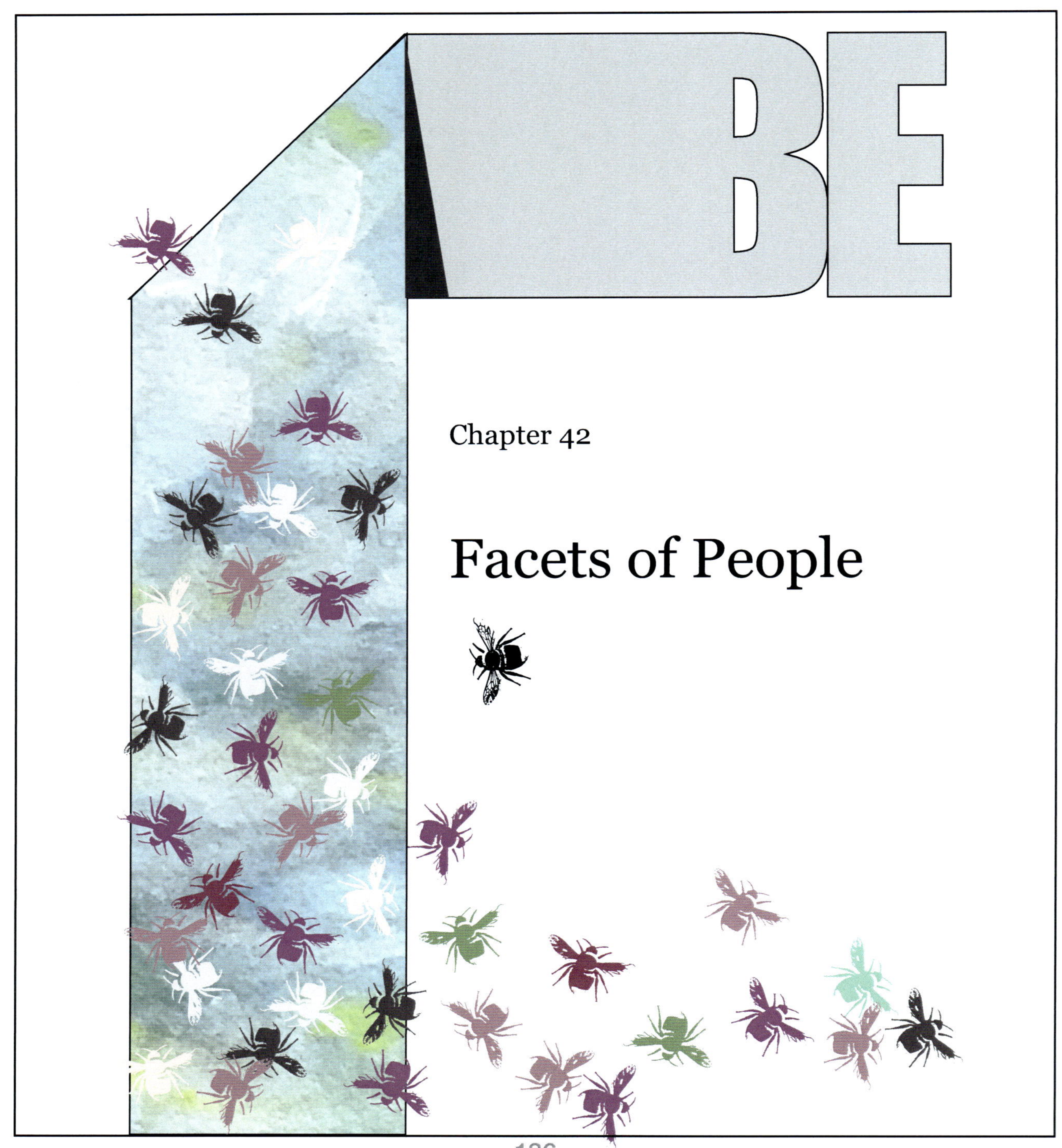

Chapter 42

Facets of People

Have you ever met someone and thought, "Wow, this is an incredible human," and then to find out there was more than this one side, and they might've surprised you, acted out of character, been mildly neurotic, or up and down like a sick cat near a bowl of warm milk?

It is because this person (as are all of us) is more than an image who we want to believe they are. There are sides to this person. They may not be the saint we thought at first meeting. No one can live up to the images others have of them.

But what's wrong with all our facets? They make life, humans, interesting, filled with inconsistencies that add character, flare, élan or "oh God," give us room for juicy gossip.

There is a part of us that is eternal, a big part of us that can bask in the eternalness of this NOW and yet, somehow we fall off the balancing wire, dive under and into the dirty water, become so much more than putting our best foot forward.

So many want us to become part of their dirty water, swim around in the tragedy of their crazed moments, become their neurosis, so often want to accuse us of their specific brand of neurosis.

And few that we meet are not in some way, on some level, lost at times in these maddening moments, these maddening days. And so it is difficult to judge a person by one action, one weakness, one interactive misconduct, on a slip up, on showing us what we think are their true colors, but really just a shade, a shadow.

We are all faceted, perplexing to live with, down right rude and crude and have sides to us that are sinister — call it evil, blackened dementia with sly smiles and yellowing teeth.

However, there is a saving grace, a certainty in all of us that can transcend it, rise above it, become more than our reactions, higher states of consciousness that we can slide into and "stay" like a good loving pet, stay securely and bring others there too, or at least hold up a road sign for them to notice.

Get not offended or confused when someone, a loved one, a new friend, an acquaintance slips into states of slithering snake-ness or lopsided neurosis and then comes back to act like the kind and gentle person you thought they were.

Seems better to always value the amazing person, no matter what philosophy, no matter what religion, no matter what career, value the person who is calm as the Pacific on a sunny day, steady as a giant ship on a small lake, as consistent as arithmetics.

We should pride ourselves, not in our emotional outbursts or in our delving into the darkness of our seemingly prescribed realities, but rather elevate ourselves in the constant NOW that we partake in, in our willingness and astute abilities to float upon any water in any storm with the salty sincerity of an old sailor, with the smile of a hound dog, with the gentleness of a fat sage after a turkey dinner, as steady as a Native American before technology ripped away their world.

So, as all people have sides to their personalities, inconsistencies, warm and cold, kind and cruel, we should accept these as merely rough edges (not as the whole part and parcel of the entire being), like youths becoming sanded down with love. And when most everyone we meet will have these protuberances on the side of the tire of their anemic philosophies, we can (as always) take what they say, how they live, the world they create with a grain of salt. We can see if there may be some holes in their perceptions, some loopholes, some areas where the water leaks through.

Few are saints, and even fewer who claim to be saints are even close to sainthood. It is usually a pretense, anyway.

Even Diogenes the Cynic walked around Athens all night with a lantern looking for an honest man, and I don't think he ever found one.

We have periods of honesty, moments of grandeur, but most slip into the darkness, become aggravated, agitated, are hard in certain unacceptable areas of their beliefs. And when they/we become adamant about a certain point, become rigid in our approaches, this is where the most work should be done. This is a place that needs to be softened with a fine cream, rubbed, opened up.

Beware of any sage. Beware of those who put you (or themselves) up on a pedestal, as most will fall off, flat on their faces and end up laughing in the gutter with a bottle of wine and a good smoke... which could be a lot more fun anyway.

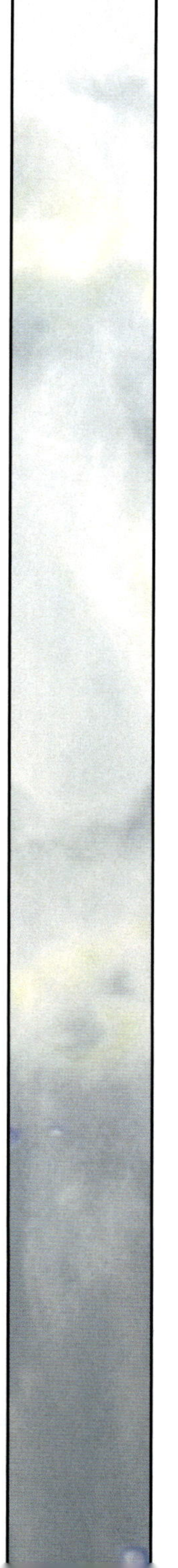

BE

Chapter 43

Do it For the Experience

So many cling to the obvious, believe force-fed concepts, adhere to social convention no matter how remote, all merely — a matter of belief.

It is safe to say, dangerous to venture to say, that life is experience. The more we experience, the greater the excitement and the more we are not fear-bound and are willing to risk that which we have worked so hard for. So the more we can see that almost any risk is no risk at all, but a perception of holding onto something that will be gently or violently or abruptly taken away anyway, then the more we can learn to live.

I once wrote: "It isn't death that scares people, it's the living that scares the hell out of most of us."

Any experience that we envision, any road that takes us to a beautiful waterfall lost in the jungle, any plane that can land us in Tahiti, any moment that we can sop up something wonderful, do it.

I would say that the greatest of sages, the wisest of guys, the most incessantly wondrous beings laying foot after amazing foot somewhere on the planet, they are the ones who can invent enlightenment in a breath, can see the surreptitious and surreal mystery in a blade of grass, can camp out with illusion and see through it all and still make it to afternoon tea, meaning: Reality, each and every moment, is wondrous and awe-inspiring.

But say you have some urge to start a new business, take some original idea and manifest it into a reality. Or say you want to save money and fly to Boise and eat a giant steak at Mani's restaurant that was there years ago, who knows, still might be there. Whatever the dream, let it be a dream.

If, as I believe, and many seem to agree, if we are living in an illusion anyway, merely a dream, then should we not suck all the juice from this dream? Should we not have fun creating new paths, creating new experiences, charging down the dark alleys, coming up with some incredulous idea and trying to make it a reality, or letting it take us for a joy ride, or not being afraid to tack, change course, breathe life into a dream that is still only an embryo, a seed waiting to germinate?

And why should we do any of this? Why should we create a dream out of a dream when all we really need to do is, in an instant, realize, "Hey this is just dream," and be blissful anyway?

I say, it gives us something to do, a new game to play. If all endeavors, all roads we go down, all pursuits, no matter how magnanimous or self-serving, are but games, then let's create our own games, envision our own rules, experience adventure when most are settling for weekly paychecks, paid health plans, and boring lunches with boring people who are so afraid to step away, to step into, to rise above, to chance it.

We are alive. We know little about the other side, about what happens to the eternal part of us (though I personally think we become one with God, with the completeness, so if we are blessed with separate consciousness, for this short period of time we should thus relish all experience in all its wondrous possibilities). And even if we, deep inside, know that we are God, and we drift back into God and will survive in some other spiritual states, why not live close to the bone, shoot flares up into the sky as some ship is sinking or passing by, or as we lead some parade down some tickertape New Year's Eve street?

If there is nowhere to get to, if we are enlightened in this forever moment (and even if we are not), does it not make sense to be able to use the enlightened moment, use this blissful state to rearrange reality, to negotiate a peace treaty with our fears, to go for it, put our beings in new experiences for the thrill of it, to reassure ourselves that we are vitally alive, we are still part of the illusion and can have some damned fun?

No matter what we do, who we do it with, no matter if we are sensing the sun as we sip coffee on the morning porch, or jumping out of an airplane and parachuting down into the azure forest, we should always try new experiences, as one would try on a new kind of shirt, as we would use excitement to force us to feel alive when the "same-old, same-old" becomes boredom on a stick, when we are like a frog in a boiling beaker, boiling slowly to death, stewing in our own stubbornness to move, until someone, something thumps the side of the jar, thumps us, and we hop out into the cool surroundings.

And maybe that is what the universe does to us, it thumps us, makes us hop out of this place into another place, drags us out no matter how much we kick and scream, gets us out of some false security into another place where we can learn, or simple enjoy or give up that which we think we must attach ourselves to.

It seems simple enough: We are enlightened this very moment. So let's take that enlightenment anywhere we choose to go and then we will never be afraid, never be anxious of what we expect or think could happen, never disappointed in what doesn't happen because we expected some result. And then we can call the earth our home, the world our oyster with a pearl, call the moment our peace, the new adventures simply a way to experience new things and have some fun. All else is clinging to states of security that do not exist, desiring things that may or may not happen, second guessing the potential of the universe when it can create entire cities from one imagination, can invent new concepts so searing and far-fetched that the most we can do is sit around with our mouths opened and gawk.

But still it is about not being rigid, or not afraid. It is about digging into the newness of each moment, leaving the known to be known and letting the unknown be not only unknown, but respected and an exciting place to venture into no matter what reality may unfold.

If we are searching for the gold buried in this undulating moment and just want to find the gold, have the thrill of looking, then when we find it, we give it away, smile and keep digging for something else we deem precious — this could be the highest adventure.

We must always be digging, even though each moment we are digging, the gold is presenting itself.

Digging is our nature. Movement is a good part of our bliss. Seeking is our excitement as we understand the seeking is but a game between having already found and tricking ourselves into believing that other things we find are simply uncovering the unknown, surprising ourselves, always being on the Easter egg hunt, realizing each and every moment is and can be a hidden egg/treasure. And if we look, we continually can see with Zen mind, beginner's mind, can witness life through the eyes of a discovering child, can be surprised by new perceptions if we are sensitive to what is passing in front of us and the newness of all things passing by...because it is always, continually, forever and ever an Easter egg hunt. It is pre-programmed into this journey of ours, a journey that has one pinpointed eternalness, yet is always taking us somewhere, some crazy creation creating.

Chapter 44

Be Not Critical

As someone once said, "A man convinced against his will is of the same opinion still."

Do we really believe we can change people's minds, show them a better way especially by being critical of who they are, what they do?

On this journey, this place of being, the incredible one-night stand that may last for 60 or 70 or 80 or more years, it is our place to do one thing over and over: Be kind. We are them and they are us and we cannot criticize our own selves.

Plus, all people have this strong thing called ego, pride, self, that doesn't like to be attacked. Attack not, and the world will surrender.

On the road to inner peace, on the high road where service and truth and giving and love are all one and the same, should we not be kind to all we meet, all who venture through our looking glass?

How can we be enlightened beings without caring for all other enlightened or non-enlightened beings?

Sure we slip up, and in our very own families, in and around our dearest friends, we become agitated, anxious, irritable — and yet society, acquaintances, are not so forgiving and understanding.

Again, it comes down to the moment, the moment which is fat with possibilities, a long-standing arrangement between all that is and all that could be. So let's be nice, polite, cordial, friendly, sincere, and never critical.

If we want to be critical, then we open ourselves up to criticism. Judge, and be judged. So on any day, in any city, on any journey, in any situation where we encounter other people, we should always be kind, as if we are seeing God in disguises trying to fool us. So no matter how the person may hurt us, let it go, be above the rabble, go beyond the foolish ways of the many to hurt, strike out, to be right, to convince ourselves of our limited points of Tightness.

Probably, on a global scale, if we could practice this one slight shift in behavior, if we (as supposedly advanced beings) can be kind and add kindness to all we encounter and be so very careful not to let our emotional response be so important and instead be calm, smile, laugh, give to the moment and anyone in the moment, then our peace will become true. Our world will become (in our minds) the wondrous place it actually is. Our day-to-day interactions with others can be one of love and caring and ease.

Not to react to the hard edges of people is just as important. We need to take the stabs and pity those who are so ready to hurt, for "they know not what they do," they are lost souls, and really they should be shot and quartered and littered across some remote island.

Just a joke.

BE BE

Chapter 45

Believe in the Magic

As the new day unfolds, believe in the possibilities, the flow, the enlightened moment to affix itself to a dream that can grow, become, flourish. If only we can help people get what they want, we can thus find joy in the unraveling.

Mankind is a creature of wants and desires. So if we can truly care about what another person wants, their real needs, sincerely help them, then the world will help us, and we can have the friends we need, the money we need. Thus, the world becomes a pleasant place where we are at home, in the peace process, caring and giving, instead of taking and self-serving.

The greatest of people were not the greatest of people because of money or stature, but because they cared, gave, developed a liking toward others.

If all are God then we should act accordingly: Help others, show them kindness, show that we can give and care and help them. And it is not a facade, or a pretense, but more of a giving because we like to care, to share, to help, to understand their trials and points of view.

But what of those who have their own agenda, care not if we live or die, only care if we can make them a profit, care only if we can line their pockets?

Walk away. There is no other choice. No matter how alluring the job, how seemingly good the employment, if he who is in charge criticizes you, blames you, tries to manipulate you with tirades, tries to motivate you for his own selfish profit, then walk away. It is better to be poor than to give to those who take, and take, until they suck a situation dry, until they aggravate the kindness of giving souls.

We must travel the path we choose. And if that path means lack of, not able to make the money we think we need, so be it. The universe comes back around. You can't keep a good guy down.

We're happy little creatures who must follow the wayward backroads, must go toward our light, create a reality that will leave a glowing wake, that will gently take us into the thickest of jungles where the mythical and legendary Emu and Anu and Oh-No live.

Gently nudge reality to come along and play, to give way. Follow a destiny, and the destiny will not let you down.

Be not afraid to ad-venture, to risk, to give to a dream, to smile as the dream ebbs and flows, as the world accepts our new ideas, as the tenuous plan collapses and leaves a shining diamond in the rough to sell for a quart of goat's milk. The magic exists, merely tap into it.

Chapter 46

The Risk Factor

There is nothing to fear, and why should we? We are in the eternal womb of God, of all things, of the eternalness, of the infinite pretending to be going somewhere.

If we proceed toward what we think we want, with love and kindness, if we give to the moment so that moment might fool us and become something, then we will be happy.

All we really want in life is happiness and peace. So if we don't feel peaceful, don't feel this sincere bliss, then maybe we should fake it. William James said, "Action seems to follow feeling, but really action and feeling go together; and by regulating the action, which is under more direct control of the will, we can indirectly regulate the feeling, which is not." Or maybe stated more simply: In order to be enthusiastic, we must act enthusiastic.

We must dream with the great dream unraveling and remember to enjoy the ride, envision greatness and be humble in our powerfulness.

For as Nelson Mandela said (really a quote by Marianne Williamson): "Our deepest fear is not that we are inadequate. Our deepest fear is that we are powerful beyond measure. It is our light, not our darkness, that most frightens us. We ask ourselves, who am I to be brilliant, gorgeous, talented, and fabulous? Actually, who are you not to be? You are a child of God. Your playing small doesn't serve the world. There is nothing enlightened about shrinking so that other people won't feel insecure around you. We were born to manifest the glory of God that is within us. It's not just in some. It's in everyone. And as we let our own power shine, we consciously give other people permission to do the same. As we are liberated from our own fear, our presence automatically liberates others."

We must have confidence that all is well this one glorious day, and any other glorious day, and this one glorious moment that goes on and on….

In truth, after all the force-fed philosophy has been spooned out, after the debates have raged, the intellectualism has sputtered and petered out, after we think we know and still slip up, after the dawn of a new day is refreshing, we finally get the one simple truth: We notice, then the world is ours. We pay attention all day long.

When we rest our mind gently and softly on the present, then we have no enemies, we can coexist with all things and walk gently and placidly amongst the stars and the downtrodden.

Enlightenment is a shift in perception, a smile, a chasing away of demons who we will not let haunt us anymore.

Enlightenment is giving and keeping a life that isn't too full or too slack, but a life where we have a wonderful mixture of peace and excitement, of a pretended future and a moment-to-moment passing that takes us to all the places we think we might ought to go.

The most enlightened ones I've met, or read, seem to be the ones who have liked themselves, the ones who can sift through the rabble and find the diamond in this purity of being, the ones who can smile, tell a bad joke and still come up with a good punch line.

We're great beyond our most intricate and wildest imaginings, but that greatness is not a pride-filled blowhard, it is not a powerful greatness where I can control the lives of a hundred men with a simple time clock.

No, the greatness is in magnanimity, in believing in all people as of great importance, as seeing each moment as truth disguised, as living with a sense of passion, with a commitment to doing something wonderful as time clicks and ticks by.

Our greatness comes from our forging our own way without fear or duress, without tacking because of a whirlwind of criticism, without yielding to authorities who seldom know.

Yes, our greatness lies in following a dream and enjoying sliding off the end of the rainbow, in using our imagination to see how things might one day be, in blissfully being in the recurring present and loving it, smiling, adding a modicum of love and peace to all situations, no matter what.

Our enlightenment comes from realizing we are enlightened creatures. For some reason we continually avoid the fact, thinking that we have not arrived, still thinking there is some place to get to.

Add love and encouragement and lavish praise to the sustenance of others, and the world will be at our beck and call, the oyster will hand over its pearls willingly, wealth will come running up to us, the truth will shine, the sun will be soft, and the wind will always be at our backs, and the possibilities will glitter all about, dancing like fireflies on some spectacular aqua evening as the full moon rises and the stars start to pop out like answers, one by one by one, to all the questions we have ever asked, finally understanding that it is all in the being, and being and being.

So as we seek, as we envision the journey we believe we surely are on, we will all come to the same conclusion: There is only one reality, one truth, one God, one point of view: Love. This book has been about one thing: How to be, realize our enlightenment, how to actualize happiness, peace.

There is nothing else, only misty facades of old buildings on some downtown, main street as the fog plays with the morning sun.

No matter how we think of a future, how we chop up reality and spit it back atcha with vinegar or spice, with sugar or lemon peels, it will always be about love, giving, sharing, adding kindness to whatever we attempt to do. It will always be about caring, doing for others as they should do unto us. It will always be the common sense of Dale Carnegie telling us to smile, never criticize. It will always be as Emerson said, “Every man I meet is my superior in some way. In that, I learn of him.” It will always be as Jesus who said, “Love thy neighbor, as thyself.” As Lao Tzu who said, “My words are very easy to understand and very easy to put into practice, yet no one in the world can understand them or put them into practice.” And it will always be as Confucius who said: “If you love what you do, you will never work another day in your life." Or as Lincoln said: "God must've loved homely people, that is why he made so many of us."

And it will always be about a little humor, and a little conversation with friends over a big plate of spaghetti as we sip a glass of wine. It will always be life, and as Tony Robbins says, "Live with passion." Or as Deepak Chopra says, "It's all about potentiality, living close to the present." Or as Ken Wilber put it so many times, "The present is the eternal moment, time is the illusion."

All say the same things, humorous things, all just drift in and out, to and away from the one thing that is self-evident: "Kindness is my true religion," said many times by 14th Dalai Lama.

We must care and love and try to give to all people, take an interest in all people, and the world will unravel like fat fishing worms in a coffee can, like a sunny day on some tropical beach as we slam down umbrella drinks. And then the world will unravel just exactly like we want it to.

There is so much to learn, there are so many intertwined in the giant ball of life, so many can shed light on things, we can learn and find small truths everywhere we go if we use the big truth of love, caring, gentleness, of being as interested in others as much as we are in our own daily little pains, and then we can use humor to explode reality into a sunset dream.

So as Yogi Berra once allegedly said, "This game is 90 percent mental, almost half the time."

Let's add a spoonful of peace to every moment, to every encounter and situation that we feel we need or want to attend to, then the world will transform itself overnight, then there will be no war, no strife, no starvation, no hunger, no problems, simply good people with sincere dreams building up and living with the one and only truth they can ever see as eternal, bliss, pure love, radiance, all walking hand in hand with God, all riding the wave of the present moment, all smiling and telling jokes and having fun in this giant sandbox of reality as all are of one common denominator: We all come from the same mud!

BE

Chapter 47

Letting Go

Why are we so adamant in our grasping onto that which doesn't want to be grasped onto? So many talk of freedom, of not being attached, of letting go, but we never know what they mean until it is our turn to let that wonderfully beautiful woman go, to let that job, that title, that belief go, to not cling to, or not grab hold of any of these things.

And ideas are just as bad to cling to as to a belief, to a concept, to a way of thinking, of acting, of reacting. This can be where most of our suffering and hardships come from.

The incredulous thing is that we are all enlightened beings getting used to and attached to stuff, then letting go of places, people, things we think we need, which gets us to the other side, to new horizons, to other wondrous things we can see into.

And what we most think of as "letting go" is not losing, is not giving something up like a mild addiction to chocolate during the full moon, or a cigar in the sweet part of a Friday drinking night. No, rather it is the releasing of our fears, creating less or no resistance to what is to become, to that which comes and goes.

It is the human condition to become expanded, taking a step into the bigger picture, going to where we are being led to go. It is this potential of the unknown that we fear. It is that which might be, that we resist and try so desperately to cling to, clinging to that which was, which need not be anymore.

Sometimes the doors to freedom are not opened wide (not quite yet), so that we can suck the marrow of the lesson.

But the doors are opened for us to go into so we can learn, find what is being taught, and then once we "get it," we get to let it go.

So no matter how much we believe we have learned, how fantastic the voyage, how incredible the present journey, we are still going to stumble across a whale-of-a-night in some seedy part of town, or we are still going to slip and fall into an abyss that will end up getting us through to the other side, so as to see the light shining in the eyes of the others we used to not even notice.

We are given relationships, jobs, circumstances, to perhaps learn from, to see through, to become one with, to smile at the involved drama going by. So let's touch what we must touch, pet the beauty, cry awhile if we must, smile and dance, drink and speak in stuttered remarks and eloquent proverbs but remember...let it go, because all things are not ours, we never get to keep any of it.

And the biggest lesson of all is how to let our own life go, watch even this flit away like a scampering butterfly fluttering and flying back out to the gentle seas of eternity.

BE

Chapter 48

Last Note

We have an obligation to give more, to care, to be enthusiastic, to realize that if we are on some kind of a journey then we might as well take chances, jump out of the hot air balloon with a hidden parachute, plan, but not be slaves to those plans. We must cry when we cry, but most importantly, see the spark of God in the little children and encourage them, breathe life into their crazy dreams, and one day as this debatable future arrives, as our innocent young ones grow into adults, they too can recall how we might've changed their lives, gave them a bone or a dream to grab hold of.

So when we all settle back into the dust from which we came, and when we speed on into the next ethereal journey, or to wherever, then we will smile across the universe and realize, "Hey, what a fine and wondrous game of life it has been."

ONE MORE LAST NOTE

There is nothing to fear but the fear of failure, fear of the unknown, fear of what could've happened, nothing to fear but the sitting around and stewing about it, thinking so much that our thinking becomes the analyzing and paralyzing inaction that aborts experience.

No matter what we believe, how we put our little world together, how we line up the sticks, no matter if the day is sunshine or rain, infamous or profane, we are surely here to "eat, drink and be merry," here to experience it...find new things to experience, new adventures, news ways to give, new trampoline rides...for life is pure sensation. So damn it, sense it, run, breathe, guffaw, cry, smile, but most importantly relish this inexplicable, miraculous and mystical experience we so commonly refer to as "our life."

Just
BE

CONTENTS art

art CONTENTS

The Greatest Investment In Your Lasting Happiness!

BE …is Available in Many Formats

- •Audio
- •PDF Digital
- •Kindle
- •Nook
- •Hard Copy, The Heirloom Edition
- •Soft Copy

There is multiple-copy pricing on www.ToBeistheanswer.com or www.GregPetri.com.

Special pricing on this unique artwork: One-of-a-kind pieces and first editions are also available.

If it is easier for you, call us direct at 303.818.2460

New Breakthrough Books by Greg Petri (check online for publication dates and pricing).

Your Two Things
Stop the Monkey Mind
Mastering Time
The Magic Portal

About the Author

Greg Petri is a fifth-generation Colorado native, raised in the small mountain town of Gunnison. Greg has run his own business, One Business Connection (1BC) since 1997, helping people actualize their dreams. One Business Connection creates and hosts inspiring events and seminars (hundreds a month!) designed simply: To inspire.

Throughout his thousands of events, Greg has met tens of thousands of entrepreneurs, enabling him to understand people and human communication at the deepest levels.

Greg has traveled in nearly 40 countries, most continents, trekked in the high Himalayas along the Mt. Everest Trail and climbed many of Colorado's 54 highest peaks. He is an avid reader of philosophy, personal development and many of the literary classics. With a degree in creative writing and English, Greg brings a different, poetic energy to his messages of peace, happiness and lasting contentment.

Greg has recorded hundreds of videos and audio programs, written nearly 20 books, and is publishing three new books in the coming year. These books (and other engaging blogs) can be found @ gregpetri.com and ToBEisTheAnswer.com.

Made in United States
Orlando, FL
17 September 2023